St Catherine's ~~Church~~
Graveyard Project

Killybegs Community Response Scheme

Published 2008 by
Killybegs Community Response Scheme
Killybegs, County Donegal

Text, images and layout by Hugh Boyle
Illustrations on pages 26,29,59 by Deirdre Keohane
Illustration on page 3 by Alison Boyle

A catalogue record for this book
is available from the British library.

ISBN 978-0-9561002-0-7

*This publication has received support from the Heritage Council
under the 2008 Publications Grant Scheme.*

*This publication is part funded by Donegal County Council under the
County Donegal Heritage Plan (2007-2011)*

*(right) 1533 - Bishop-Elect Quintinius O Higgins blesses the waters off
Killybegs after the Herring and Sprat disappeared.*

Killybegs LTI Supervisors

Hugh Boyle : Research
Philip Kemp : IT Instructor
Brendan O Donnell : Video Instructor
Edward McClafferty, Mary Robinson

Trainees who assisted with the book and CDROM

Michael O Shea, Mary Carr, Mary Cunningham, Siobhan Mc Brearty, Catherine Lyster, Brid O Keefe, Mary Rouiller, Thomas Maguire, Marcella Breslin, Lisa Conroy, Karina Quigley, Emer Mc Hugh, Ciaran Mc Hugh, Carmel Lyons, Elaine Hardy, Carmel Brennan, Aidan Mc Closkey, Brenda Hardy, Loretta Shovlin, Jessica Adair, Gareth Moore, Mairead Mc Hugh, Tanya Mc Guinness, Oliver Smith, Rachael Cassidy, Laura Keeney, Patrick Breslin, Dennis O Donnell, Bernadine Boyle, Catriona Mc Cole, Emma Mc Hugh, Maria Doogan, Angeline Wilson, Agnes Cunningham, Elaine Murrin, Linda Gallagher, Emma Gough, Kevin Ryan, Fionnuala Cunningham, Anne Marie Shiels, Helen Bourke, Sheila Diver, Peter Callaghan, Alan Mc Brearty, Anne Marie Byrne, Anne Breslin, Nicola Rowan, Aidan Mc Morrow, Nigel Dowds, Yvonne O Gara, James Mc Mahon, Paul Gavigan, Aileen O Doherty, Mary Gillespie, Maire Curran, Deirdre Keohane, Freda Gillespie, Sinead Byrne, Enda Murphy, Leanne Gillespie, Mark Lafferty, Gerard McBrearty, Shay Murrin, Shane McBrearty, Elaine Diver, Deirdre Doherty, Peter Ward, Gemma Byrne, Tom Hegarty, Ann Carr, Charles Tully, Claire McShane, Brendan McGuire, Katherine Gallagher, Bernadette Herron, Roisin McNelis, Sinead McNern, Frank Gallagher, Marie Hennigan, Connell Gallagher, Kevin Cunningham, Stephen Muirhead, Charles Henry, William Johnston, Maire Geraghty, Sandra Down, Colm Sweeney, Mary Martin, Mark Long, Eunan McIntyre, Kathy Hegarty, Matthew Smith, Joanne O Donnell, Barry McFadden, Damien Carr, Eddie O Donnell, Jason O Boyle, Sharon Jones, Noelle Jones, Mathew Jose, Elaine Gallagher, Marian McGinley, William Hegarty, Liji Jose, Catherine McHugh, Dixi Patterson, Theresa McMenamin, Carmel O Toole, Jennifer McMenamin, Laura Breslin, Aine McGinley, Lorraine McNern, Bernard McHugh, Siobhan McNamara, Mary Gallagher, Denis Coleman, Veronica McDaid, Edel Gallagher, Deirdre McIntyre, Donal O Brien, Kevin McCloskey, Margaret Breslin, Liam Carroll, Sean O Donnell, Ann Marie Carr, Joan Moore, Evelyn Cunningham.

Table of Contents

Foreword

I am delighted to be associated with this highly professional production, providing an interactive history of St Catherine's Church and Graveyard. This is a very impressive and thorough piece of historical and archaeological research and is an important contribution to the local historical archives. St Catherine's Well, which is situated right beside the church and graveyard, is an active site of pilgrimage, not just for the people of Killybegs but for pilgrims throughout the country and indeed from abroad. St Catherine's Church and Graveyard is an important historical and religious site and I sincerely hope that the launching of this wonderful production will inspire a sustained effort to save the remaining structure from ruin. My warmest congratulations to Hugh Boyle, supervisor and driving force of the project, Philip Kemp, Brendan O Donnell, and the FÁS Community Response Scheme trainees on their outstanding achievement.

Is ábhar bróid agus dóchais do phobal na gCealla Beaga go bhfuil and taighde cuimsitheach seo foilsithe anois. Tá súil agam go mbeidh ar ár gcumas anois an láthair stairiúil eagasta seo a chaomhnú. Comhghairdeas ó chroí leis an fhoireann uilig a thug an tógra seo chun críche.

Fr. Colm Ó Gallchóir, Parish Priest, Killybegs. October 2008

Foreword

For many years the ruins of St Catherine's Church and Graveyard lay unnoticed with its most frequent visitor being the ravages of time. Part of our history was disappearing before our eyes, a Church that was a beacon of Christian witness since the 15th century seemed certain to keep her secrets forever as the Church ruins deteriorated and the gravestones disappeared under flora and vegetation.

This treasure house of local history and religious heritage has been uncovered, recorded and magnificently presented by the successive participants of the FAS Community Response Scheme set up in 2001.

The hours of research, the painstaking detailing of headstones and Church structure, the contextual story told of a developing community have been worth it all. We owe these young people and their supervisors a great debt of gratitude both as a Community and a Church for putting us into context, helping us to find our place in history and making us aware that we stand on the shoulders of those who have gone before and encouraging us to reach a little higher.

Rev. Ken McLaughlin
Rector of the St John's Church of Ireland Church,
Killybegs. 2008

Introduction

Killybegs has many stories; stories of pirates, priests and planters; stories that have shaped lives near and far; famous stories and half-forgotten stories.

This book and accompanying DVD tell a story in stone. A story that began before the time of St. Patrick and has links to many different threads in this community.

The little church of St. Catherine of Alexandria has stood on a shoulder overlooking Killybegs harbour since at least the fifteenth century. Just a few yards away, the Well dedicated to the Egyptian saint continues as a place of daily pilgrimage.   But the church and its surrounding graveyard - unused and uncared for - has largely slipped from community memory so that many barely know of its existence.

The work of many hands has gone into the telling of this story. Sponsored by FÁS, the national training and employment authority, a research project has spent seven years studying the old building, examining the gravestones, and carrying out investigations as far away as Belfast to uncover the information of the stones. We hope that this work will appeal to many people at many levels.   It is, essentially, a work of history, but there are also records of the flora and fauna of the old graveyard and fascinating detail about the lives and times of those who are buried there and the lives they led.

Having studied the old church and cemetery, it is hoped that the structure of the church can be saved from collapse. It is in a delicate condition with ivy and small trees rooting in the walls.   But experts advise that it can be saved if the will – and the money – are there.

But that's another story.

ST CATHERINE & KILLYBEGS

St. Catherine and Killybegs
Life of St. Catherine

The tradition of St. Catherine in Killybegs has long been an important aspect of the town and one that still continues to be very strong in the area today. Killybegs is quite unusual from other areas in southwest Donegal, in that, it is not a local saint that is venerated, but an early saint from Egypt.

It is believed that St. Catherine was of noble family and of exceptional learning[1]. St. Catherine converted to Christianity during the reign of the Emperor Maximinus II (308AD –313AD)[2]. Maximinus tried to woo Catherine, but she was openly hostile to him because of his anti–Christianity. Maximinus engaged her in a debate where he had 50 philosophers challenge her on the Christian church. Catherine not only defeated their arguments but succeeded in converting all the philosophers to Christianity. Maximinus enraged by their failure to defeat Catherine had the philosophers burned alive.

Catherine turned down an offer of marriage from the Emperor, which resulted in imprisonment and beatings, but this was not to have any effect on the young saint who during her incarceration succeeded in converting Maximinus's wife and two hundred soldiers to Christianity. The Emperor then had Catherine put over four wheels joined together with sharp pointed spikes, that, when the wheels moved her body might be torn to pieces[3]. As the torture began the wheels broke apart and killed and injured many of the spectators, after which the Emperor finally ordered to have her beheaded. Legend has it that when she was beheaded milk instead of blood flowed from her veins.

St. Catherine's body was removed from Alexandria and taken to Mount Sinai in Egypt sometime after the Saracens captured the city in 642AD. The monastery of St. Catherine still survives today on the Holy mountain on the Sinai Peninsula.

St. Catherine and Killybegs

The exact period of history in which the cult of St. Catherine was introduced into Ireland and Killybegs is somewhat obscure and of considerable academic argument. St. Catherine is not mentioned in Western Europe before the eight/ninth century[4] and it was with the returning crusaders in the twelfth/thirteenth century that the cult of St. Catherine gained mass popularity.

The historian Dr. Myles Ronan states that the Normans brought devotion of St. Catherine to Ireland in the twelfth Century[5]. However some scholars believe that there was connection between early Christian Ireland and the early "Coptic" Christian church of Egypt via Spain and the western seaboard and it is possible that it was these Egyptian monks who brought the cult of St Catherine to areas of Ireland. The Tau Cross on Tory

Island, the "bed" dedicated to St. Catherine on Lough Derg and Kilnaboy in Co. Clare are suggested as evidence of this "Coptic" connection. It may also be important to note that the Normans never held any authority over Killybegs or Tír Conaill.

The popular story of the introduction of the cult of St. Catherine to Killybegs is more widely known. "A party of monks were making a voyage on the west coast of Ireland"[6]. The boat was caught in a great storm and the crew prayed in desperation to St. Catherine "patron saint of seafarers" to protect them and bring them safely to shore and they vowed that if they reached land they would dedicate a holy well in her honour. They arrived safely in Killybegs harbour and dedicated the well to St. Catherine.

The medieval area of Killybegs shows the importance of which St. Catherine was held at that time. The remains in that area contain St. Catherine's Church, St. Catherine's Well and Kits' Castle or Cats' Castle, which is undoubtedly a contraction of St. Catherine's Castle[7]

The earliest documented evidence of Killybegs' relationship with St. Catherine is an entry in the Annals of the Four Masters in the year 1513. The entry describes a raid by three ships under Eoghan O Malley on Killybegs and the retribution they received for the sack of the town.

1513

Owen O'Malley came by night with the crews of three ships into the harbour of Killybegs; and the chieftains of the country being all at that time in O'Donnell's army, they plundered and burned the town, and took many prisoners in it. They were overtaken by a storm on their return, so that they were

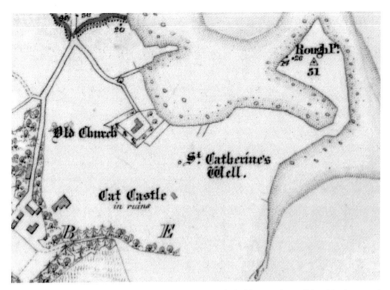

The first known map showing St Catherine's Well, Reproduced by kind permission of the Ordnance Survey of Ireland

compelled to remain on the coast of the country; and they lighted fires and torches close to their ships. A youthful stripling of the Mac Sweenys, i.e. Brian, and the sons of Brian, son of the Bishop O'Gallagher, and a party of farmers and shepherds, overtook them, and attacked them courageously, and slew Owen O'Malley, and five or six score along with him, and also captured two of their ships, and rescued from them the prisoners they had taken, through the miracles of God and St. Catherine, whose town they had profaned.[8]

St. Catherine is still very much revered in the Parish of Killybegs as well as in the surrounding parishes. In Killybegs today, St. Catherine gives her name to the local soccer team, the secondary school, as well as various other businesses and houses. The feast day of St. Catherine (November 25th) sees many people from the area and beyond come in constant stream from dawn to midnight[9] to take part in the pilgrimage to St. Catherine's Well.

ST. CATHERINE'S WELL

Know ye the town in Donegal?
Tis Killybegs Fairest of all.
Surrounded by hills and mountains so grand,
And Harbour so safe - where ships loved to land.

Know ye the story told to us all?
Of a ship in great danger near Donegal?
Waves lashed around her like mountains so high,
And flashes of lightening appeared in the sky.

The sailor's last hope was a prayer, which they said,
With a promise to Heaven if to safety it led,
That a well to St. Catherine they'd dig in the soil,
Of the land which to safety they'd try hard to toil.

St. Catherine stood at the helm, guiding them over the foam,
And prayers were raised to Heaven from sailors far from
home,
And so to this well in thousands we go, each year to pray
For Peace from all woe - On good St. Catherine's Day.

Written by Josephine McLoone Cleary (1875-1959) The
Diamond,
Killybegs. She was the youngest daughter of Neil McLoone
and his
Wife Elizabeth.

From: Phil Hogan, Rathfarnham, Dublin

Holy Wells

The origins of holy wells in Ireland probably date from the pre-Christian period. A source of clean and pure water was, on a physical level, an important life sustaining resource, while on a spiritual level it was a link between the real

Statue : St Catherine's Well

world and the "other world". With the coming of Christianity the sacred places were blessed for the new religion. The people who would return to these sacred places no longer visited pagan shrines but Christian ones.

St. Catherine's Well is located between the ruins of Kits Castle and St. Catherine's church. It is still held with reverence by both the people of Killybegs and of the surrounding parishes. It is still a place of daily pilgrimage for many people.

History and Folklore of the Well

The story of the monks who had been caught in a storm and upon safely reaching shore through the miracle of St. Catherine is the only early story that exists about the well.

It is not known about the status of the well during penal times and the practice of worship would hardly have been encour-

The crystal clear waters of the well

aged, if allowed at all. However no specific folklore survives from this period. Towards the end of the eigtheenth century the Catholic Church itself discouraged the practice of praying at holy wells, and the persons that came were careful to hide the fact from the priests[10]. The Catholic Church condemned pilgrimage days such as the 25th of November around 1800AD. During the famine the people then returned to these old sites to pray to the old saints for relief from hunger, disease and starvation.

It must have been this return of large numbers of pilgrims that incensed the Church of Ireland Rector William Lodge in the 1850's who decided to take action to stop the practice. The following story appears in the Derry People in 1928.

THE FILLING OF THE WELL

"Tradition has handed down a curious incident associated with the well. Probably about 70 years ago (1858) the Rectory was occupied by the Rev. Mr. Lodge, who was then the Protestant Minister of the parish. Apparently possessed with a singularly narrow mind and completely devoid of the spirit of religious tolerance, he was much perturbed by the sight of so many people praying day after day at the well. The Rector took steps to prevent this by erecting strong fences everywhere there was a likelihood of tres-

pass. *The people avoided the grounds, but the numbers at the well showed no diminution. St. Catherine's Day, with its crowds, seemed to have raised the ire of the Rector to breaking point. On the day after he ordered a number of his workmen to accompany him to the well. Under his supervision, the well was filled with earth and stones and probably the worthy man returned to his home self-satisfied in having up an end to at least one "Romish" custom. Next morning, his drawing room, though situated on an eminence at a much higher level then the well, was flooded with water from no conceivable cause. His wife, who, it is said, had a strain of catholic blood in her veins, grew hysterical and pleaded hard with her husband to undo the work of the previous day. Finally yielding to her entreaties, he consented and the employees were dispatched to re-open the well. The water in the drawing room immediately subsided and from that day until his death, no interference with the well or its devotees ever took place.*

Probably half a dozen Rectors have since then occupied the house but, to their credit be it said that not one of them possessed the characteristics of the Rev. Mr. Lodge in this respect"

Station of St. Catherine's Well

Begin by kneeling and saying the following:

For those who opened the well.
One Our Father
One Hail Mary
One Gloria

In honour of St. Catherine.
One Our Father
One Hail Mary
One Gloria

For the priest who blessed the well.
One Our Father
One Hail Mary
One Gloria

Begin the Rosary.
Say the Creed
One Our Father, three Hail Mary's and Gloria.
Take three sups of water from the well.
Go around the well three times saying a decade of the rosary each time.
Kneel and finish the Rosary.

End by praying for your own intentions.

How the well has changed

The earliest photograph of the well is from the William Lawrence collection and taken sometime between 1905 and 1910. It shows St. Catherine's well before the surrounding wall was built. The well is almost completely surrounded by a mound of stones

and the well itself is made of larger stones. The layout of the well in this photograph is probably what the well looked like for hundreds of years.

In the 1920's, a considerable sum of money for the purpose of making a path from the road to the well was sent by a native of

Killybegs to the parish priest Dean Sweeney. The Dean organised voluntary help from the parishioners to construct a path, which is still the main access route to the well. During the

construction of this path a number of coffins were un-earthed, which is proof that the graveyard walls do not mark the boundary of burials around the church.

It may have been at this time that the modernisation of the well begins to take place. A postcard from the mid-1930's shows that considerable work had been carried out on the well. The mound of stones surrounding the well has been levelled and were probably used to build the familiar wall surrounding the well. The gate was put on a short time after the wall was built to prevent animals from using the well. The physical change in the well from this work was substantial and we begin to see the makings of the modern well. The area inside the new walls is levelled with concrete.

The next photograph taken in the 1960's shows the addition of the grotto containing the statue of St. Catherine.

The well and surrounding area has continued to be improved by the people who use it on a daily basis.

St. Catherine's Church

St. Catherine's Church is located to the south of Killybegs on the west side of Killybegs harbour. Its position is probably located in the area adjacent to the medieval town of Killybegs.

The main body of the church was built in the 1400's possibly by Mac Swiney Bannagh for the Franciscan Third Order Regular[1]. The Third Order enjoyed an expansion in the west and North West of Ireland in the 1400's, particularly in Donegal in the second half of this century. By 1500 five Franciscan Third order houses had been founded in Donegal[2]. There is no concrete evidence however to state when exactly it was built and for whom. The origi-

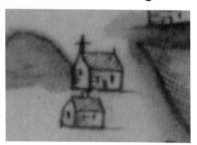

St Catherine's Church from the Phillips Map of 1622

nal chapel consisted of the nave and the chancel.

The chancel was traditionally always placed at the east end of Church, and was the location of the altar and also reserved for the clergy. The Nave located on the west side of the chapel was where the laity stood to partake in the mass. There are no windows surviving in-situ from the period. The only surviving feature is the blocked-up doorway on the south wall of the chapel. It is the presence of this doorway that allows the building to be dated. The door, which is of gothic style, has chamfered jambs and an exterior chamfered head-mould. The door is undoubtedly an original feature and is of a fifteenth century character. It must be remembered when looking at this doorway that the level of the out- side ground was much lower than today's level. Four hundred years of

Original doorway of the church, the style dates from the 15th century

burials has raised the ground substan- tially.

Although none of the original windows survive in-situ, parts of the windows do exist.

Windowsill from the church

In the graveyard is a windowsill, which is of a similar rock to that of the door. This window- sill fits the approximate dimensions of the window openings in the front of the chapel. By examining this windowsill, it is possible to reconstruct what these windows may have looked like. It is clear from the sill that it was a single light with chamfered jambs. The windowsill also has a pivot hole for a shutter, which means the window did not have

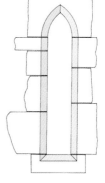

Reconstruction of window

St Catherine's Church

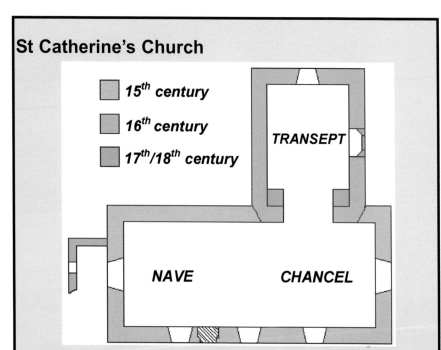

- 15th century
- 16th century
- 17th/18th century

TRANSEPT

NAVE   CHANCEL

This plan of St Catherine's church shows the different periods of additions and alterations carried out on the structure of the building. These additions and alterations enable the building to be read like a book. By looking closely at the stonework on the building it is possible to see what was built first and what was added on later and by looking at the stone-cut features it is possible to give a date to the additions. When there are few early historical records available for a building such as this, this method can provide the only means of looking into the distant past.

The picture on the right shows the punch-marks on the arch that leads into the transept. The style is from the 16th century (the 15th has lighter punch-marks and the 17th is much heavier). This allows us to date the transept as being built in the century after the nave and chancel was built.

glass, but had a wooden shutter, which would only allow light to enter if the shutter was open. There are no remains left of the head or lintels of the windows, but it is likely that they were in gothic style like the doorway and could have been carved from a

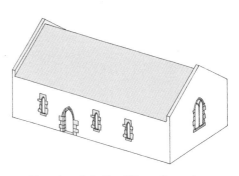

The church in the fiftheenth century

single piece of rock, which is typical of churches in the fifteenth century. The window, which would have been above the altar, would undoubtedly have been larger than the front windows. Another windowsill rebuilt into the window of the later built transept contains a reused window sill[3]. It is possible that this was used originally for the chancel window. A carved-out hollow in the middle of the slab denotes that it had a mullion or upright pillar splitting the window into two sec-

St Catherine's Church and the enchanted land of Hy-Breasail

The story of Hy-Breasail and its link with St Catherine's Church is told in the excellent book written by a Killybegs teacher Thomas C McGinley in 1867 called *The Cliff Scenery of Southwest Donegal*. The story talks of a beautiful enchanted land inhabited by the faeries that appears from time to time close to the coast of Rathlin O Byrne island before becoming enshrouded in a mist and disappearing.

The young Mac Sweeny and crew approaching the enchanted land.

After many fruitless attempts by locals to reach this land an old wise man was consulted. The old man said that the person who had the power to capture this enchanted land had not yet been born and he would have special marks on his body. The old man said this Mac Sweeny would have to let a crow fly over the land to make it visible to the human eye and then throw a burning coal and some earth onto the land to claim it for the human race.

A young Mac Sweeny who fitted this description was born a short time later in Teelin. Knowing he had the power when he became older he gathered a brave crew and set off to capture the enchanted land. When they were near Rathlin O Byrne he released the crow. The crow flew west and almost immediately a large and beautiful land appeared from beneath the sea. The land stretched as far as the eye could see with luscious pastures with flocks of sheep and herd-sof cattle. Little fairy-like people played like excited children and on seeing the approaching boat and its strange-looking crew ran down to the beach to satisfy their curiosity.

Mac Sweeny and the crew manoeuvred the boat to a bank that was adjacent to the beach and as they approached they noticed two large rams fighting. The little people, still intrigued by the crew followed quickly in the direction of the bank. As the men threw the anchor, a red-haired lady who was knitting on the bank above them dropped her ball of golden thread into he boat. The lady drew up the thread and the boat lifted out of the water and then releasing the thread the boat crashed back into the water. The frightened men held on to the boat as she repeated this process until one of the men grabbed the ball of thread to throw it from the boat but the ball attached itself to the mans hand and the boat started to lift and crash even more violently. One of the other men took his axe and cut off the hand holding the ball sending it into the sea. While this was happening the two rams had continued fighting during which one of the ram's horns broke off and landed in the boat. The crew regained their senses and went to complete their task but the tossing of the boat had extinguished the coal and washed away the earth that they were supposed to cast onto the   enchanted   land.

They knew now that their task had been a failure and so left and returned to Teelin. In the bottom of the boat they discovered the horn that the ram had lost during the fight. Afterwards the horn was hung up in St Catherine's church *"where it remained till a period not very remote, and was constantly referred to as furnishing ocular evidence of the reality of Hy-breasail, the enchanted land."*

tions. As with the previous sill, it contains a pivot hole. If this sill was used in the original chancel window it would have made quite a narrow window of approximately 450mm in width, much smaller than the existing opening of this window. However we know that this window was enlarged in 1793 at a cost of £1-10-0[4].

The sixteenth century

The sixteenth century saw the addition of the transept onto the church. This may have served as a sacristy or something similar as most transepts join onto the nave or between the nave and the chancel. Again we have no precise date or record for this addition.

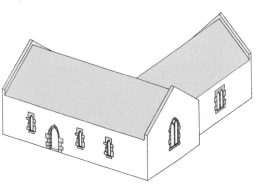

the sixteenth century church

The entrance to the transept is through a dressed stone arch. The dressing on the stone has been identified as being of sixteenth century style[5]. When the transept was originally built it appears that the roof members joined on to the original roof. The second arch here was not built until later. It is unclear what the level of the ground outside this transept would have been at the time of building.

Everyday life in the church is unclear to us from this period. We do not know how many clergy would have been involved with the day-to-day running of the church. The Annals Of The Four Masters state that the town of Killybegs was plundered and

The Spanish Armada in Killybegs 1588

In 1588 a Spanish force set off to conquer England. After a disastrous defeat in the English Channel, the Spanish ships fled northwards. Many ships were lost off the coasts of Scotland and Ireland. Three ships managed to reach the safe harbour of Killybegs but two of these sank inside the harbour and the third and largest managed to land safely but with some damage to its hull and rudder. The crews of the Girona and the other two wrecks stayed in Killybegs until they had repaired the Girona. By this time Don Alonzo de Leiva and the crew of the ship called the Duquesa Santa Ana that had foundered of Loughros Point near Ardara had joined them. Don Alonzo, who was second in command of the entire Armada, took charge. On the 26th of September 1588 the Girona left Killybegs with over 1300 men on board. With no more room on the ship, hundreds of Spaniards watched from the shore as their compatriots sailed off to Scotland. On the 28th October the Girona struck a reef off the Antrim coast. Out of the entire crew, only nine men survived. It is the worst maritime disaster connected with Killybegs.

burned twice in this century. The first event was in 1513 when Owen O' Malley of the infamous pirate clan from western Connaught pillaged the town and captured many prisoners at a time when the fighting men of the area were away with O' Donnell's army. Brian, the young son of the Mac Sweeny chieftain and others attacked the O' Malley's and rescued the prisoners. This account states that this was through the miracles of God and St. Catherine, whose town they had profaned[6].

Drawing of the transept window showing much rebuilding, more possible evidence of the turbulent 17th century,

The second time was in 1550 by Rory Ballagh Mac Sweeney who, in retaliation for not receiving the lordship of Tir Bannagh from Manus O' Donnell, "went to Killybegs, and totally plundered that town"[7].

This gives us a good insight into the period of the inter-clan skirmishes that were typical in Gaelic Ireland and church property was not exempt from this plundering. With the O' Malleys incurring the wrath of God and St. Catherine, it is possible that his plundering extended to the church.

These entries in the Annals also give the picture that Killybegs was at this time an established town, probably on account of the profitable fishing industry at this time, which was a corner stone of Tír Conaill's wealth. Towns in areas that had not been conquered by the Normans or Vikings such as Tír Conaill's, were rare as Gaelic Ireland was essentially a rural place.

Another significant event later in this century was in 1588 when ships and crews of the Spanish Armada landed in Killybegs. Around 1500 Spaniards waited in Killybegs while the Girona was being repaired. Some of these, such as the Commander of the land forces of the Armada, Don Alonso de Leiva, had already survived being shipwrecked twice, firstly on the "La Rata Encoronada" on the Mayo coast, and then again five days later, on the Duquesa Santa Anna in Loughros Bay, near Ardara. These men must have attended the church during the period they stayed in Killybegs before the subsequent and fatal journey on the Girona.

Towards the end of this century the Nine Years War was under way. The Gaelic Lords of Ulster were in constant battle with Queen Elizabeth's forces.

The Seventeenth Century

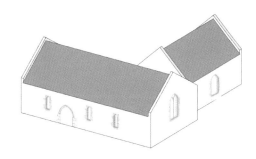

The failure of the Ulster Lords in Kinsale on the 3rd of January 1602 and the subsequent Flight of the Earls in 1607 signalled the end of the Gaelic order. Ulster was now open for English conquest and all its lands were forfeit to the

The church became the property of the new Church of Ireland. The second arch and gable was built in this period as well as the blocking up of the main doorway.

crown. In 1609 an inquisition was held at Lifford to determine the size of church lands in Donegal. With this established, all church lands became the property of the protestant Church.

Killybegs was to become a corporation town with Roger Jones being giving the task of setting it up. One of the conditions required by the charter was that a church had to be provided for the new community of "Planters". St. Catherine's Church proved to be a convenient building for the small new community and the church was converted for Protestant worship in 1615. The Church must have been repaired at this time because it was described in 1622 as being 'newly re-edified and well repaired.

This could suggest that the church was damaged in the aftermath of the Nine Years War although there are no historical records to confirm this.

It is possible that this was the period when the south transept arched gable was built to remove the weight of the transept roof from the sixteenth century arch. The new arch contains cut stone from other parts of the chapel. This could also be evidence that the church had been severely damaged.

17th century arch showing the location of re-used cut stone. This would suggest that there had been severe damage to the church

James Hygate became the first protestant vicar of Killybegs in 1609[8] . Robert Hamilton became the first rector in 1622. Hamilton is a name that was prominent in Killybegs since the initial phase of the Plantation. It is likely that Robert Hamilton was the rector at the outbreak of hostilities in 1641; there is no record of what happened to him.

The 1641 Rebellion was an attempt by the remaining Irish nobility to regain the lands and power they had lost over thirty years previously. In the early days of the rebellion, a fierce battle occurred at Stragar, about four miles from Killybegs. The Irish forces under Turlogh Roe O'Boyle of Kiltoorish, and the sons of the late (and last) Chieftain of Bannagh, Donough McSwyne, were routed by the forces under the Reverend Andrew Knox. There is no record of a second battle, but in 1642, Colonel Mervyn admits that the English Forces evacuated Killybegs. The Irish immediately filled the vacuum left by the withdrawal of the English forces. The Franciscan friars from Donegal took advantage of this and settled into the church. A number of these friars were captured in Killybegs by an English ship that came in disguise and succeeded in capturing Father Ultach and Father Fergal Ward. Father Ward was hanged about three months later while Father Ultach was brought to England and paraded through different towns in his Franciscan habit before dying in prison shortly afterwards.

By 1648 the town was back in the hands of the English forces and the friars had fled again. St. Catherine's church again was back in protestant control. This troubled period may have again damaged the church as the 1654-56 Civil Survey showed that the church was in repair.
The remainder of the seventeenth century in Killybegs was quiet; the turbulence of 1690 seemed to have very little impact in the area. The only link surviving from the latter part of the century is the grave of John Lindsey, dated 1685.

The Eighteenth / Nineteenth Century

The eighteenth century in Killybegs was a much more settled period than the previous century. The town was by now firmly in the control of the planter population who took advantage of the peace to develop trade and fishing. The new town of Killybegs was now the main area for development and commerce and only the church remained in the old medieval town

Baptismal font dated 1717

Fortunately there are a number of historical records throughout this century concerning the church. In 1729 the Bishop gave one hundred boards for seating. In 1733 the church is described as in good order, seated and the aisle and altar flagged with stone. A baptismal font was donated to

Another view of the baptismal font. 1717 is visible on the lip. This is the only piece of architecture surviving from St Catherine's Church.

the church in 1717 and is now located in St. John's Church. Unfortunately its inscription is very difficult to read and only the date is legible. It is the only known surviving furniture from St. Catherine's Church. It was decided in a Select Vestry meeting in 1788 to re-slate the roof of the church. The new roof was completed in 1790 under the supervision of James Hamilton and Andrew Nesbitt at a cost of £15. Further work was carried out in 1793 to enlarge the chancel window, which cost £1-10-0. In

1795 the road to the church was improved with a new pipe drain. Two new sash windows were installed on the church at a cost of £1-16-6; it is still possible to see traces of the sash frames in the remaining plasterwork on the church[9].

By the beginning of the nineteenth century, the Church of Ireland had commenced an impressive church building programme through the Board of First Fruits. Money was secured by the parishioners and in 1825 building began on a new church located in the new town, a much more convenient location than St. Catherine's. By 1828 the new church was complete and was dedicated by the Bishop on the June 6th.

After religious worship for over five centuries St Catherine's Church was now abandoned. Burials continued in the graveyard but the last living link with medieval Killybegs was severed.

St Catherine's Church today in the 21st century is in a very poor condition. It is the oldest surviving building in Killybegs and a window into over five hundred years of our history. If it continues to be ignored as an important and valuable resource then the town will lose it forever.

THE GRAVEYARD

St. Catherine's Graveyard

The ancient graveyard of St. Catherine's that surrounds the church has been used by both denominations throughout the centuries. It is an important part of Killybegs historical heritage and thus should be treated with respect.

One of the main aspects of the project was to carry out a comprehensive survey of the graveyard and record all that we found. This included:

- Gravestone inscriptions;
- Scale drawings of Gravestones;
- Exact locations of Gravestones;
- Types of Gravestone;
- Flora and fauna of the Graveyard;

Felix O' Neill had carried out a survey of the Graveyard inscriptions in 1986[1]. However, this was incomplete. He had recorded 39 gravestones in his survey so we began by verifying the inscriptions in his survey and then recording the remaining gravestones. To do this, we had to remove vegetation from most of the gravestones to read the inscriptions. This was performed in compliance with the regulations and approved methods laid down by Dúchas. This is important because insensitive cleaning could easily damage the stone, thereby destroying the inscription forever.

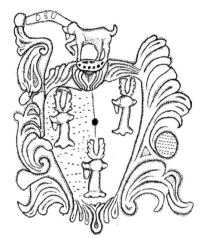

Greenlaw Crest

While some of the gravestones' inscriptions were relatively easy to read, others required much perseverance on behalf of the trainees, for example the grave of Patrick Finision required almost a full week to decipher its inscription. The removal of mosses from a large number of gravestones was required and this was achieved using water and a soft bristle brush in compliance with Dúchas and FÁS guidelines. The inscription survey recorded 57 inscriptions and a number of other graves, which were impossible to read. The earliest surviving gravestone in the graveyard is that of John Lindsey who died in 1685. It is located inside the church so it is impossible to locate his grave accurately. The last burial to take place in the graveyard was V. H. Lavery a Stoker onboard HMS Corncrake, which disappeared in stormy seas off the Donegal coast while escorting a Canadian Royal Naval convoy to Gibraltar in January 1943. The most important discovery during this survey was the grave of Patrick Finision Provost of the corporation town of Killybegs who died in 1703 and will be discussed later.

Gravestone Crests & Symbols

The different types of crests on the gravestones can be broadly divided into three categories

Religious and Symbolic

The most common form of decoration is religious symbols. This example has a Celtic cross surrounded by a sun. The letters IHS are an abbreviation of the name of Jesus Christ.

Family Crests

There are some finely carved family crests on a small number of gravestones. Only the more prominent families in the area would have their crests displayed. This example shows a stag's head that is part of the Greenlaw family crest. Other fine examples include the Nesbit and Hamilton tombs.

Secular Decoration

Secular crests appear on only two gravestones in the graveyard. This crest from the Patrick Finison tomb of 1703 probably represents the Corporation of Killybegs as he was the Provost. The other is the World War Two grave of V. H. Lavery.

The next phase of the survey was to complete scale drawings of each individual gravestone recording the following information:

- Type of memorial;
- The shape and dimensions of the memorial;
- The stone type;
- Any decoration or symbols;
- Any mason's name, mark or address;
- The condition of the memorial;[3]

Types of memorial:

There are four types of gravestone memorial in St. Catherine's Graveyard;

Slab or Recumbent Slab

The majority of gravestones are of this type. The slab gravestone is simply a rectangular slab of rock, which lies flat on the ground. It is not clear if the earliest gravestone of John Lindsey (1685) was of this type.

Asken / Brown 1742

Slab tombs appear to be the earlier type of memorial used in the graveyard with it being the principle type used until around the 1820's. The type of stone used in these memorials is a significant contributing factor on the present condition of the gravestones. Only one of the inscriptions on the limestone slabs have been preserved, the others are unreadable due to the spalling of the rock. The problem with using a soft rock for this type of memorial is that

it can become saturated in wet ground, which invariably caus-
es the layers of rock to break apart especially during freezing
weather. Loughros slate is a hard durable rock and where this
has been used the inscriptions, carving and even the masons
guiding lines have remained sharp and clear as the day it was
carved.

Table Tombs:

Blain 1848

Table Tombs are the logical development of slab memorials. This
memorial consists of a slab similar
to the above, but raised on four
stone legs, i.e. a table. The table
tomb is a much more visible type
of memorial than the slab and was
popular in the late eighteenth to
the mid nineteenth centuries. The
advantage of a table over a slab is
that with a slab being raised from
the ground it is less susceptible to
damage from moisture. It also
allowed the mason to create deco-
rated edges around the slabs and
to decorate the legs, which held it up. In order for the mason
to achieve proper proportions for this memorial, a thicker slab
than the previous memorial was necessary. Sandstone and a
coarser form of sandstone, locally called Millstone grit mostly
from the Mountcharles area were the most suitable rock types
for these table tombs.

The earliest example of a table tomb in the graveyard is that of
Michael and William Brice (1781-85). It is in poor condition but

still contains moulding around its edges. Fine examples of Millstone grit table tombs are the Blain tombs of 1847 and 1848. The inscriptions and features on these tombs are still sharp due to the hardness of this rock but this hardness also limits the artistic aspirations of the mason, and are finished much plainer than their finer grained "Freestone" counterparts.

One of the major drawbacks of the table tomb is its stability. Due to ground settlement after burial and the passage of time the footings of these tombs become uneven giving it the characteristic lopsided look, which all the tombs have. This can lead either to the collapse of the tomb or to the fracture of the slab as is visible to the McGhee tomb (1815).

Box-tombs:

The Box-tomb is the most elaborate form of memorial in the graveyard. The Box-tomb is similar to the table tomb but is completely enclosed below the raised slab. There are three examples of this type of tomb but unfortunately all have since collapsed. The earliest tombs belong to the Hamilton's of Fintra (1815,1817). These tombs, built in classical style, incorporate six carved legs, which resemble corner pillars and pilasters enclosing six panels to enclose the tomb.

Panel from Hamilton Box-tomb 1811

Another panel found in the graveyard has a round classical detail carved on it, and is probably from one of the Hamilton Tombs. This type of tomb can still be seen intact at the old Killaghtee graveyard near Bruckless, and dates from a similar period to that of the Hamilton graves.

The other Box-tomb in the grave-yard is that of Mary Kelly who died in 1869, the wife of Hugh Kelly who was an important busi-nessman in Killybegs in the mid 1 8 0 0 ' s .
Again this tomb lies collapsed and the base uneven due to ground subsidence. There is a box-tomb at St. John's Church of the same design, which remains intact and is dated 1868 and obviously the work of the same mason.

Box-tomb from St John's Church 1868

4.   Upright memorials (Headstones)

The upright memorial is self-explanatory. In its simplest form it consists of an upright slab of rock with the inscription facing the   grave.
 The upright memorial has been used in Ireland from at least the early Christian period, the earli-est of which can be seen in the south west of the country and the inscriptions are written in

Jones 1819

"Ogham", the earliest form of written Gaelige.
 The earliest surviving upright in the graveyard is that of William Henry Atherton (1837), a simple memorial that has remained in good   condition.

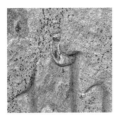

Fossil on the Laphel memorial

Another upright, that of Sarah Elis Laphel possibly dates from 1838 and again is of a relatively simple design. This memorial is made of a soft limestone and was placed with its natural layers placed vertically. This has allowed the penetration of water between the layers, severely eroding the memorial and destroying much of its inscription. However one interesting feature of the Laphel memorial is the presence of small cockle type fossil, which lived in the shallow tropical sea that existed here over 300 million years ago.

From the second half of the nineteenth century the upright becomes the prominent type of memorial in the graveyard. A number of these memorials have collapsed. The later uprights came from the Drumkeelan area of Mountcharles. The styles of these vary from the simple finishes to more substantial constructions such as the Meighan memorial. The upright erected in memory of V.H. Lavery, a stoker on board HMS Corncrake, which sank off Donegal in 1943 was the last memorial to be erected in the graveyard. It is a simple limestone slab with an anchor crest. Unfortunately it was recently cleaned in a very poor manner.

Other Grave Markers

Carved stone memorials were obviously only available to those who could afford such an expense. There are a number of plain stones on the periphery of the main burials, marking the graves of people unable to afford a permanent personal memorial. The relatives of the deceased would have known

Grave marker

these marker stones but sadly the names and dates of such people have been lost over time.

Another form of memorial that would have undoubtedly been used in the graveyard would have been a wooden cross. This type of memorial can be seen in the early photographs of other graveyards in Donegal in the early 1900's. As wood is a perishable material, nothing survives of these and the location and number of individual graves is now not known.

Stone Masons

There are a number of memorials in the graveyard, which appear to have been carved by the same stonemasons. However we are only certain of one stonemason by name. Patrick Quinn was a stonemason at the mines at Drumkeelan and examples of his work can be seen in graveyards all over the south and west of the county. Patrick was responsible for the carving of the Greenlaw (1902) memorial and is typical of his style. Patrick, who had a passion for botany, would sketch different wild flowers and foliage, and incorporate this floral theme on most of his work[3].

Angel : Morrison 1826

The mason responsible for two of the Loughros slate slabs may possibly be Thomas Mulhern from Cashel, Ardara. Grave slabs by Mulhern can be seen in graveyards all over southwest Donegal. They usually contain a carving of the face and wings of an angel and are quite primitive in style. His later

46

works contained some very abstract designs.

Stone Type

The different types of stone used in the memorials can be divided into the following basic divisions.

Asken/Brown Crest 1742

Loughros Slate

Loughros point appears to have supported quite an industry in the manufacture of gravestones in the eighteenth and nineteenth centuries. Gravestones of this clean bluish rock can be seen in a large number of old graveyards including Templecrone, Iniskeel, Glencolmcille, Killaghtee, etc. This is a hard durable rock and has lasted much better than the other rock types used in the graveyard. The type of gravestones that Loughros slate is used on is predominantly of the slab type, and all examples in this graveyard are of this type. Loughros slate was used at one time for roofing, which was called Boylagh slate, but by the time of T.C. Mac Ginleys Journey in 1867 its use was confined to paving purposes[4].

The earliest gravestone of this stone in the graveyard is that of Mary Brown (1742) and its decoration and inscription is still fresh and easily read. Indeed after a period of over 260 years even the mason's guiding lines are still visible.

Sandstone

There are two distinct types of sandstone used in the grave-yard.

Millstone Grit

Greenlaw 1902

This is a coarse form of sandstone from the Mountcharles area where it is known as "Sugar Granite". This type of rock is used on uprights, slab tombs and box tombs and the earliest known grave of that material is that of Capt. James Murray (1752). As the grains in this rock are quite large, it is difficult to attain fine detailing. All the graves of this type of rock are quite plain with very little or no decoration.

Mountcharles Sandstone/Freestone

Mountcharles sandstone or freestone would have come from the Drumkeelan mines, the only site in Ireland where this stone was mined. This mining was apparently initiated c.1174 by Cistercian Monks to get ornamental stone for Assaroe Abbey in Ballyshannon[5].

Freestone is capable of being carved in any direction and the mason is able to create intricate designs. The skill of the Drumkeelan masons can be seen in many graveyards throughout the area as well as St Eunans' Cathedral in Letterkenny and the National Museum in Dublin.

Limestone

Limestone was used for a small number of graves, and all the stones are in poor condition. Only on two of the gravestones is it possible to read the inscription, and on one recently discovered gravestone it was only possible to read "ge Blain" – possibly George Blain (the third George Blain in the graveyard). Limestone is a soluble material and can deteriorate quite rapidly in wet conditions. It is not known the precise location of the rock but T.C. McGinley noted in 1867 that in Ballymacdonnell near Dunkineely "there are several excellent quarries of dark fossiliferous limestone... is considered to be of a very superior quality"[6]. However, limestone is quite common along Donegal bay and the stone used in the memorials could have come from any of these places.

Limestone upright
Lavery 1943

No.	Name	Year	No.	Name	Year
1	Murray	1752	32	Hamilton	1813
2	Finison	1703	33	Kelly	1869
3	Montgomery	1806	34	McLaughlin	1837
4	Asken/Brown	1742	35	Unknown	
5	Teelin	1785	36	Dobin	1784
6	Atherton	1837	37	Unknown	
7	Jones	1819	38	Devenny	1740
8	Mathews	1858	39	McCloskey	1850
9	Greenlaw	1902	40	McCloskey	1818
10	Blain	1792	41	O'Boyle	1808
11	Blain	1848	42	McGill	1847
12	Blain	1847	43	Laphel	1838
13	Blain	1777	44	Mc Intyre	1832
14	Blain	1721	45	Gallagher	1856
15	McGhee	1815	46	Mc Hugh	1816
16	Banks	1807	47	Morrison	1836
17	Mitchel	1840	48	Carr	1847
18	Greenlaw		49	Morrison	1826
19	Black	1783	50	Conwell	1847
20	Unknown		51	McLean	1857
21	Gay	1784	52	Meighan	1857
22	Nesbit	1719	53	Kennedy	1856
23	Magee	1812	54	Kennedy	1855
24	Magee	1804	55	Conwell	1817
25	Henderson	1836	56	Quinn	1858
26	McDoel	1801	57	MaGinnis	1841
27	Hamilton	1817	58	MaFadien	1806
28	Hamilton	1815	59	Pallock	1833
29	Hamilton	1811	60	Brown	1847
30	Brice	1781	61	Lindsey	1685
31	Lavery	1943			

Graveyard layout of St Catherine's Church

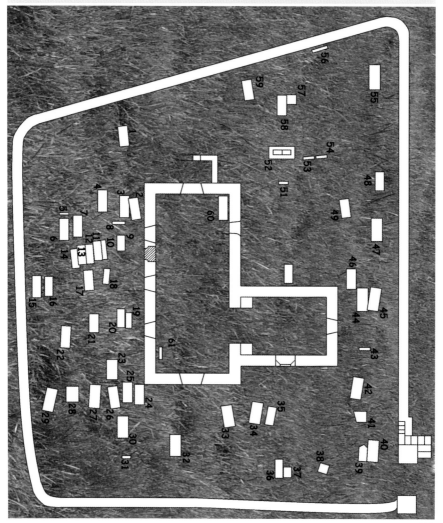

Scale drawing of the Meighan Memorial 1857
All measurements in millimetres

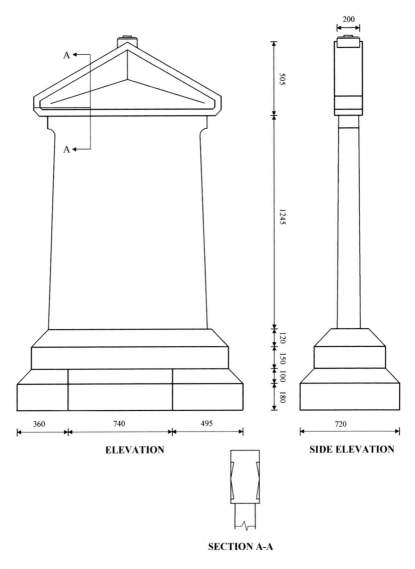

ELEVATION

SECTION A-A

SIDE ELEVATION

THE CASTLE

Kit's Castle

Kit's castle is probably a corruption of "St Catherine's Castle". It is superbly situated on a prominent hill overlooking Killybegs

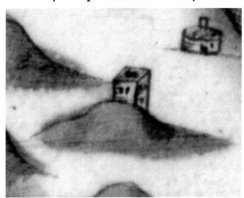

harbour, and is directly above St Catherine's well. It was built around 1355 by a native of Killybegs, the then Bishop of Raphoe Padraig McMonagle. A manuscript in the British Library tells us that "*Patrick Magonyell made an appointed three manner houses (beside the Bps sea) for the Bp of Rapho, vizt Portlyna at Banbeltay, Tyre kerren which was the Bps mensal and Killwarrfine at Buncarran and killbarrfine together with the Courte of Killbegge at bunfarcannaght which was [ ] likewise a mensall*"[1].

Kit's Castle from the Phillips map of Killybegs 1622

Padraig Mc-Monagle was from the Erenagh family of Killybegs. An Erenagh family in Gaelic Ireland was the family who traditionally were the hereditary keepers of church lands like the Breslins of Inishkeel, the O'Duffys of Templecrone or the McNelis family of Glencolmcille. The Church owned extensive lands in Ireland at this time. The reason Bishop Mc-Monagle may have built these three manner houses was to strengthen the Church's hold on its land. The previous Bishop of Raphoe, Bishop Thomas Mac' Cormac O'Donnell had given his consort, Honora Mac'Sweeney, the church lands of Tir Mac'Caerthainn,

Kits Castle is situated above St Catherine's Well.

lying apparently between Kerrykeel and Ramelton[2]. Bishop Mc Monagle was probably trying, though unsuccessfully, to reclaim these lands for the Church. There are no remains or tradition of a manor house in this area.

The other manor house he created was at Killbarron on the southern extremity of the Diocese of Raphoe. This is probably the castle destroyed in 1390 by Donnell O Conner on the site of the future O Cleary Castle[3]. It would appear then that the remains of Kit's Castle is all that remains of the three manor houses erected by the Bishop.

The castle was not used after the plantation and subsequently very little remains of it. The walls of the castle in 1847 were approximately 7ft wide, the internal measurements of which are 17 1/3 ft x 14 1/6 ft. It is not known how tall the castle was, but it was probably two or three storeys high. Directly on the west side of the castle, the remains of a foundation of a rectangular structure or wall that was connected to the castle are visible. The castle was described in 1867 as having a "long flight of stone steps leading up to the main building from the ground below on the side farthest from the sea"[4]. On the 1907 Ordnance Survey Map, a ramp is clearly visible leading up to the castle on this side verifying that the entrance was on the west side, but the stone steps have long since disappeared. The trace of foundations on this side could have been a form of a court or a yard adjoining the castle.

The builder of Kit's Castle, Bishop Patrick Magonyell died in 1366[5]. Kit's Castle was occasionally occupied by other Bishops after this. In 1533 the Bishop-Elect Quintinus

Bishop-elect O Higgins blesses the water of Killybegs and the fish return.

O Higgins arrived in Killybegs by boat from Sligo. Killybegs, then as now, relied on fishing, as it's main industry. O Higgins was "disappointed to find that bay, which formerly teemed with herrings and sprat, then completely deserted by fish"[6]. The inhabitants earnestly requested that O Higgins help them from this misfortune and "yielding to their solicitation, he persisted in his supplications to God, until the former abundance of fish re-appeared in the bay at the point where he had imparted his blessing"[7]. Fish was a cornerstone of the medieval economy in Tir Connaill. Fish was exported to the continent in great quantities from Donegal, which earned the O Donnells, as overlords of Tir Connaill, great wealth in royalties as well as being known in the continent as "Kings of the Fish". Quintinus O Higgins then stayed in Killybegs becoming popular with both clergy and laity. O Higgins also became a good friend of the ruling O Donnell chief, of Tir Connaill Hugh Dubh at the time, but O Higgins criticism of Hugh Dubhs marriage led to his expulsion from Tir Connaill and subsequently was never consecrated as Bishop of Raphoe.

The next resident of note was another Killybegs man. Donald Mc Gonigle was also a member of the Killybegs Erenagh family. Donald visited Rome in 1560 and on his return was chosen as a companion for the Apostolic Delegate to Ireland, Father David Wolfe. Their task was to visit some of the most disturbed parts of Ireland and report back to Rome on the true conditions of the state of the church in Ireland. Father Wolfe initially sent letters describing their findings but decided that it would be better to send Donald McGonigle to Rome to give first hand reports.

The letters that Mc Gonigle took to Rome included a recommendation from Father Wolfe to the Pope that Patrick Mc Gonigle be made Bishop of Raphoe. This was carried out in 1562 and one of the first duties the new Bishop had to participate in was to join the two other Irish representatives at the

ETIAM · IN · MEMORIAM ·
ILLUSTRISSIMI · ET · REVERENDISSIMI · DONALDI · MAC · GONIGLE ·
EPISCOPI · RAPOTENSIS · UNUS · EX · TRIBUS · EPISCOPIS · HIBERNICIS ·
QUI · AD · VARIAS · SESSIONES · SACROSANCTI ·
CONCILII · TRIDENTINI · PIO · IV · PONT · MAX · INTERERANT · OBIIT · 1589 ·
APUD · KILLYBEGS · SEPTEMBRIS · 29 · IN · BENEDICTIONE · ERIT · MEMORIA · EJUS ·
ERECTED · BY · THE · PARISHIONERS · 1866 ·

Plaque in St Mary of the Visitation Church, Killybegs, commemorating the towns most illustrious son.

Council of Trent in the north of Italy. This was a great honour for the Killybegs native and he performed with distinction and described as *"the flower of his age"*[8].

At the close of the Council he quickly returned to his diocese which was know in a very unsettled state due to the succession wars of Calvach and Sir Hugh O Donnell. It may have been because of this that Bishop Mc Gonigle decided to make Kits Castle his permanent residence and he spent the rest of his life living there while walking a political tightrope between his ever increasing rebellious fellow county men and the expanding English authorities intent on gaining power in the northwest. The Bishop died on the 29th of September 1589[9].

Born in Tirconnell around 1545, Niall O Boyle was educated in Spain. While still in Spain he already had come to the notice of English spies who described him as dangerous in their reports back to England. On his return back to Ulster he was installed as Parish Priest of Iniskeel before being consecrated Bishop of

Raphoe in 1591[10].

The beginning of the Nine Years War in 1594 between the Ulster Gaelic Lords and Queen Elizabeth saw increased activity in Kits Castle. Bishop O Boyle was an ardent supporter of Red Hugh O Donnell and rigid opponent of English rule in Ireland. Almost immediately Kits Castle became a place of intrigue, the Bishop was in constant communication with Spain, and his every move was being watched by English spies and known to Dublin Castle. In 1596 Bishop O Boyle wrote to the King of Spain thanking him for the aid he was about to send. In the same year he was host to Alonso de Cobos, an envoy from the King of Spain. It is reported that O Boyle was captured by

Bishop Niall O Boyle, ardent supporter of Red Hugh flees Kits Castle after the defeat of the Ulster forces in Kinsale in 1602. This was the last time a Bishop resided in Killybegs.

Very little remains of the little castle that played an important part in a crucial period of Irish history.

the English forces in 1597 and suffered imprisonment and torture. However this did not deter the rebel Bishop and in 1600 he provided hospitality to Ferdinand of Barranovo and the Archbishop of Dublin, Matthew de Oviedo and the main topic of discussion was no doubt Spanish military aid for the ongoing war.

The Battle of Kinsale and the subsequent defeat of the Ulster Lords was a crushing blow to O Boyle. Because of the high level of involvement by the Bishop, Kits Castle was no longer a safe haven for O Boyle. One night in 1602 he slipped away from the castle and Killybegs to take refuge in the ancient holy site of Disert in the Bluestack mountains and he spent most of his time between here and the castle of Kiltoorish near Portnoo until his death on the 6th of February 1611. Bishop Niall O Boyles body was carried north over the hills and buried on Iniskeel Island, another ancient holy site.

FLORA & FAUNA

Flora And Fauna

The flora and fauna of the area surrounding the Church and Castle was surveyed on a continual basis throughout the duration of the project. This area proved to be rich in the diversity of plants and animals.

Initially, part of the area was tidal, but the new pier development has covered over this. The area between Church and Castle is now situated a considerable distance from the sea. Consequently a number of the types of flora and fauna recorded in the early stages of the project are no longer present.

Herb-Robert

Chaffinch - path to church

Starting at the entrance on the Roshine road and continuing in the direction of the Church brings you past the old sewage treatment works. The area is now just waste ground, but contains a small number of trees and a variety of flowers. On most days, small numbers of songbirds may be seen here, the most common being the *chaffinch*. *Goldfinch* congregate here in small numbers and their striking plumage may be observed as they fly from tree to tree.

As you continue walking, keep an eye out for another small bird called a *dunnock*. This shy bird looks similar to a sparrow but can be identified by its lead-grey head.

The low ditch on the right hand side of the path contains a variety of flowers including *bitter vetch, herb-robert* and *navelwort* which are visible from May until July when they are overgrown by *yellow vetchling, marsh willowherb* and a type of *st. johns-wort* called *tutsan*.

The path now splits into two directions. The path leading to the church will be taken first. The area to the left of the path is mostly dense scrub with *common gorse* (locally called *whin bush*) and which pro-vides important cover for small birds such as *robin, wren, and song thrush*. The old ditch on the right hand side of the path is quite shady due to the *hawthorn* bushes that grow above it. Leaving the gate

Wood Sorrel - path to church

towards the church, the ditch in late spring is covered in *wood sorrel*, a delicate flower with lilac-veined petals and drooping shamrock leaves. Standing here observing these will usually incur the wrath of the resident *robin* whose "tick-ick…" call is telling you of its annoyance and for you to continue on. In springtime the lower part of the ditch you will find the small

flowered *golden saxifrage*. As spring progresses into summer a variety of flowers can be seen such as *st. johns-wort's, herb robert, lesser stitchwort* and small white flowered *enchanters night-shade*, which grows beside the steps of the gate.

Rustyback Fern - graveyard wall

Standing at the gate you can now see most of the graveyard and church. The graveyard is a good haven for wildlife. Ancient graveyards such as these have not been sprayed with weed-

63

Green veined White - graveyard

killer or improved with artificial fertilisers, thereby ensuring that the variety of plant life remains, which in turn attracts insects, birds, and mammals.

The wall surrounding St. Catherine's graveyard was built in the early 1800s, the large sycamore trees growing around the wall were probably planted around this time also. The graveyard wall supports a number of plants. The lime mortar provides nutrients for these plants to grow. Ferns include common *polypody*, the delicate *maidenhair spleenwort*, *hartstongue*, and the small fern *rustyback*. A flower, which thrives on this wall, is *navelwort*, the circular leaves of this plant are visible from early spring and in summer produces a tall white flower.

Opposite-leaved golden saxifrage dominates the floor of the graveyard in springtime along with the yellow flowered *lesser celandine*, a flower that thrives in many graveyards. At the southern side of the graveyard the flower *lords and ladies* grows in abundance and it may have been planted on a grave because it does

Bee on dandelion

not grow outside the graveyard nor would it be common in this a   r   e   a   .
As summer progresses, the small flowers such as *bittercress,*

cuckooflower and *dandelions* begin to be overtaken by the larger flowers.

Yellow Iris grows mostly on the eastern side of the graveyard, while the rest of the graveyard is dominated by *meadow-rue, nipplewort* and *hogweed*. Several types of *vetches* use these plants as support by wrapping tendrils around the growing stems of the plants and are lifted up with the plants as they grow.

Large White on blue-bell

The church provides an unlikely habitat for trees. *Sycamore, ash* and *hawthorn* seem to thrive on top of the walls and the strength of their roots is clearly visible as they slowly push the walls apart. The eaves of the church have a nice display of *primroses* in early spring and *perforate st johns-wort* grows on the north-eastern side of the transept. Inside the church *common figwort, woundwort* and *burdock* grow in abundance due to the sheltered nature of the site.

Wood mouse - Graveyard

The graveyard provides a haven for bird life. *Wrens* are common sight here and nest among the vegetation. In the summer of 2001 a *spotted flycatcher* nested on the little porch and its aerial displays while catching insects was a spectacular sight. Sadly the location it had chosen for its nest was not suitable and the eggs were destroyed before they could hatch. *Thrushes* have also used the transept area for nesting but a predator also destroyed their eggs.

A *great tit* for its nesting sight used one of the doorways of the church. It used a hole through which the nest was safe from predators and was frequently observed flying into and out of this hole with food for its young chicks.

Perforate St John's-wort - church wall

The *wood mouse* is the only known resident mammal in the graveyard. This mammal is quite tame in summer where it can be approached to within a close distance, where it is usually feeding. Another mammal known to use the graveyard is the *badger*. This is most noticeable in winter when the telltale signs of the small holes in the ground, which are made by the badger foraging for insects, are visible.

The flora and fauna of the graveyard and church should be explored at a leisurely pace and the observant eye will find much of interest here. To continue the tour, return back to where the path splits in two and now follow in the direction of St. Catherine's Well.

Hogweed - graveyard

The ground to the left of the path had a large hedgerow of large mature *field roses* but these were sadly removed in 2002. The bank on the right has a number of interesting plants such as *yellow pimpernel* with its delicate five-petalled flower, *forget-me-nots, bog pimpernel, slender st. john's-wort*, as well as more basic plant forms such as *mosses* and *liverworts*.

Swans off Smooth pt.
14/10/02

When the long metal railing are reached it is difficult to imagine that at one time the sea came in to where you are now standing. This tidal bay was a good place to watch wildlife. A pair of resident *grey wagtails* could be seen most days, identifiable by a flash of yellow and their wagging tails. When the tide was out numbers of wading birds such as *redshank, oystercatcher* and *turnstone* used the area for feeding. Seagulls also used the area and occasionally rare gulls from the arctic such as *glaucous* and *iceland gulls* could be seen here.

With high tide, this little bay was used by other sea birds such as *shag* and *cormorant*. Swans and *common seals* also were occasionally seen. Plant life adapted to salt conditions occurred by the shore such as a large type of daisy called *sea mayweed* and *scurvy grass* which was used in years gone

Small Copper feeding on Devil's Bit Scabious - beside well.

by sailors in the belief that it could prevent scurvy. This has all disappeared under the new pier development and only a pair of hooded crows seem to have adapted to this progress. The filled-in area has been planted with a "wild flower mix" and

Foxglove - path to well

plants such as *poppy* and *sweet alison* now grow here. None of these plants are native to this area.

Moving on to the gate, the rock outcrop on the right is a good place to view ferns such as *hard fern, polypody, scaly-male, hay-scented buckler fern*, and *black spleenwort*.

Approaching St Catherine's Well by the steep path listen carefully for sound of the *sedge warbler*. This visually shy bird was only heard during the survey but never actually seen. Other birds to be seen here are the *linnet, starlings*, and *greenfinch*. The damp pastureland between the well and castle contains a variety of flowers including two orchids, the *common spotted orchid* and the *heath spotted orchid*. These two are beautiful flowers and quite similar looking and it is worth the effort spending a little time to distinguish the difference. The blue flowered *devils bit scabious, black knapweed, ragged robin*, and a variety of buttercups provide good feeding for numbers of butterflies. The tiny but brightly coloured *small copper* is regularly seen here, as well as *meadow browns, ringlets* and *orange tip*.

On reaching Kit's Castle you are rewarded with a panoramic view of Killybegs. Directly below you is the church and well, which along with the castle constitutes the medieval town of Killybegs. In the distance can be seen the modern town of Killybegs that has developed since the Plantation of Ulster. The high mountain of *'Cronarad'* dominates the view to the west and the harbour lies to the east.

English Stonecrop - Kit's Castle

The walls of the castle provide a home for *oxeye daisy*, which has large white flowers and the small patch that grows here is the only place where it grows within the survey area. Other plants include *yarrow, black medick, nipplewort* and *black spleenwort*. The floor of the castle is overgrown in summer with *common nettles*. The *holly* tree growing to the southwest of the castle has another noisy resident *robin*.

Black Spleenwort - Kits Castle

The steep slope to the south of the castle has an interesting number of plants. The delicately flowering *english stonecrop* appears to grow directly out of the bare rock. Below this several different types of *speedwell* grow side by side. Most of the flowers here require you to get down on to your knees and inspect them at close quarters; these include the unusual looking *eyebright* with its numerous colours. This is also a good area for butterfly's; look out for the large and brightly coloured *peacock* butterfly. Retrace your steps to the well and exit either by the new pier or return the way you came in.

Willow Warbler - graveyard

Dunnock - graveyard

ROUGH POINT

Rough Point/Smooth Point

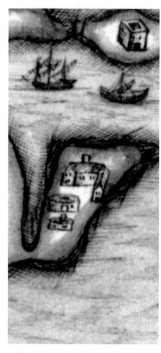

Rough Point : Detail from the Phillips map of 1622. The castle at the top is where Mooneys boat yard stands presently.

Rough Point was a tidal island located at the west End of Killybegs. It is believed that this area was part of the Medieval Port of Killybegs; it was in the vicinity of Kit's castle, the Church, and the site of McSwyines Castle in Castlepoint.

Due to the proposed development of the new pier in this area and Rough Point being identified, as an area of archaeological significance it was required that archaeological excavation be carried out before any development took place. Archaeological Development Services carried out a preliminary excavation in 2000. This identified the remains of three stone built structures on the upper part of the island, while a possible larger structure, tentatively identified as a manor house, was identified on the lower eastern part[1].

Aegis Archaeology Limited undertook full excavation in August and September 2001. Each building was excavated by hand and the remainder of the island was striped of topsoil in order to discover any other archaeological remains.
The excavation revealed the remains of five separate buildings, a tethering stone, the remains of a boundary wall and an area

of "Lazy beds" or cultivation ridges.

The findings from the excavation suggest that these houses possibly date from the early seventeenth Century. This would mean that the buildings date from the initial period during the plantation of Ulster.
 The building although in very poor condition provides us with a valuable insight into this type of housing during this period. This excavation is of importance because there has been very little excavation of this type carried out in Ireland from the plantation period or from the Gaelic ruling period preceding it in relation to dwellings. Further excavation of this type could reveal the development of traditional housing and the influence that the building techniques the early planters brought with them had on the changing lifestyle of the native population during this period.

The buildings on Rough point show some of the characteristics found on Irish dwellings such as the opposite doors on the structure 5 and the rounded corners on structure 2. There are however features incorporated in these structures that could not be classified as typically Irish. This is most evidently in the construction of the fireplaces. On structures 3 and 4, the fireplaces are built into the corner of the gable wall instead of the centre. Two of the fireplaces in structures 3 and 5 are built as outshots, i.e. built on the outside of the gable. Structure 3 also has a cobbled area spanning the width of the room at the opposite end of the gable, which evidently was also used as a fireplace.
The structures at Rough Point may mark the end of old Gaelic timber and wattle building traditions, and the beginning of a different, more solid structure, which ultimately formed the blue-

print for what is recognised today as vernacular Irish building[2].

Structure No. 1

Structure No. 1

This building measured approximately 13m x 5m. It does not appear to have been used as a dwelling. The existence of large drains at the bottom of the house suggests that it may have been used for livestock.

Structure No. 2

The second building was of similar size to structure No. 1 but different in style. Whereas structure No 1 had sharp corners on the gable, structure No. 2 had more rounded corners, typical of the Irish style of construc-

Structure No.2

tion. The floor at one end of the building was flagged with stones. Incorporated into this floor were two broken rotary quern stones. Rotary quern stones were used for the milling of grain and have been in use in Ireland until the 20th Century.

Structure No. 3

Higher above the two first build-ings, the remains of two other buildings were discovered. The layout of the ruins is roughly rec-tangular although the main walls are slightly curved. The house contained a large   fireplace in the south corner gable, which was built as an outshot from the gable wall. The space beside the fireplace may have been

Fireplace : Structure No. 3

used for a bed. An alcove was recorded on the right hand side of the door; this could have been the location of a dresser or possibly a bed. The opposite gable had a small are flagged with stones. There is evidence that this was used as a fireplace but there is no sign of a chimney in this end of the house.

Structure No. 4

This building lay close by and at a right angle to building No. 3. Only three walls were surviving at the time of excavation. The surviving gable end contained a fireplace off-set from the centre allowing a space between it and the north wall. This presumably would have been an area for sleeping similar to that contained in thatch cottages

Structure No. 4

surviving today.

Structure No. 5

Located on the Southeast side of Rough point were the most intact remains, consisting of a rectangular structure with an internal stone partition. The rooms each had a fireplace on the gable walls. These fireplaces both consisted of a cobbled hearth. The chimney on the south side of the house was built into the gable as an outshot possibly

Structure No. 5

utilising the space either side of the hearth as a sleeping area.

East fireplace : Structure No. 2

The other fireplace consisted of a square cobbled area placed against the gable wall. As in structure 3 there appears to be no chimney built to carry the smoke away. It could have utilised a wattle chimney but more likely the fire was just built against the wall and escaped through a hole in the roof. This possibly enabled the owner to avoid having to pay the tax for two hearths thereby making a saving of two shillings.

The house appears to have had two doors opposite each other

although the door facing the sea had being blocked up at some time. This two-door layout is very common in Irish traditional buildings and is still seen on thatched cottages today. It is believed the purpose of these two doors was to regulate the draught for the fire, which may have previously been placed in the middle of the room on the floor. The fireplace was possibly moved to the gable end, thereby reducing the need for the two doors.

The floor in this room had several flagstones on the floor and this may indicate that the whole floor was flagged.

The archaeologists discovered while excavating this house that it had burned down and that the roof had collapsed during this fire. Initially, it was thought that there might be artefacts concealed underneath this but there was nothing found when excavated. This suggests that the house was uninhabited at the time of burning and that the house had being cleared of everything before departure.

Tethering Stone

This was discovered collapsed between structure 3 and structure 5. A groove ran around the top of the stone, possibly worn by the action of a rope. This would have originally been in standing position and could possibly have been used for tying an animal.

Tethering stone

References

Chapter 1
1. Livingstone, E, *The Oxford Dictionary of the Christian Church*, Oxford University Press, USA, 1997.
2. Mallon, M, *St. Catherine's Well*, Dearcadh, Ardara, 1994-95
3. Mallon, M, *St. Catherine's Well*, Dearcadh, Ardara, 1994-95
4. Conaghan, Charles, *The History and Antiquities of Killybegs,* pg 24, Ballyshannon, 1974..
5. Conaghan, Charles, *The History and Antiquities of Killybegs,* pg 24, Ballyshannon, 1974.
6. Lacy, Brian, *Archaeological Survey of County Donegal,* pg 304, Lifford, Donegal County Council, 1983..
7. AFM – *Annals of the Kingdom of Ireland by the Four Masters, from the earliest period to the year 1616,* 7 Vols, Dublin, 1856.
8. Conaghan, Charles, *The History and Antiquities of Killybegs,* pg 24, Ballyshannon, 1974.
9. ibid.
10. MacGill, P. J, *The Parish of Killaghtee*, p6, 1968.

Chapter 2
1. Gwynn, Aubrey and Hadcock R Neville, *Medieval Religious Houses, Ireland,* London, 1970.
2. Conlan, Fr Patrick, *The Franciscan Third Order in Donegal,* Donegal Annual, 1997
3. Lacy, Brian, *Archaeological Survey of County Donegal,* Lifford, 4. Donegal County Council, 1983.
4. Conaghan, Pat, *Bygones,* Killybegs, 1989
5. Lacy, Brian, *Archaeological Survey of County Donegal,* Lifford, Donegal County Council, 1983.
6. AFM – *Annals of the Kingdom of Ireland by the Four Masters, from the earliest period to the year 1616,* 7 Vols, Dublin, 1856.
7. AFM, *ibid.*
8. Conaghan, Charles, *The History and Antiquities of Killybegs,* Ballyshannon, 1974.
9. Conaghan, Pat, *Bygones,* Killybegs, 1989

Chapter 3

1. O Neill, Felix, Graveyard Inscriptions – St Catherine's, Killybegs, 1986.
2. Doran, Linda, FAS Graveyard Guidelines, 1990.
3. Per Comm. Eamonn Monaghan.
4. Mac Ginley ,T.C, The Cliff Scenery of South-Western Donegal, pg 165, Reprinted by Four Masters Press, Dublin, 2000.
5. Centenary Committee, Cententary of The Church of the Sacred Heart, pg 37, Mountcharles, Ballyshannon, 1997.
6. Mac Ginley, T.C. , The Cliff Scenery of South-Western Donegal, pg 26, Reprinted by Four Masters Press, Dublin, 2000.

Chapter 4

1. Jefferies, Henry A, *A catalogue of the bishops of Raphoe to A.D. 1600*, pg 108, Donegal Annual, 1997
2. Silke Fr John J, The Diocese of Raphoe, pg 27, Catholic Church, Diocese of Raphoe, Letterkenny, 2000.
3. AFM – *Annals of the Kingdom of Ireland by the Four Masters, from the earliest period to the year 1616,* 7 Vols, Dublin, 1856.
4. Mac Ginley ,T.C., The Cliff Scenery of South-Western Donegal, pg 45, Reprinted by Four Masters Press, Dublin, 2000
5. AFM – *Annals of the Kingdom of Ireland by the Four Masters, from the earliest period to the year 1616,* 7 Vols, Dublin, 1856.
6. Maguire, Rev. Canon Edward, A history of the Diocese of Raphoe, pg 112, Browne and Nolan Limited, Dublin, 1920.
7. Maguire, Rev. Canon Edward, A history of the Diocese of Raphoe, pg 113, Browne and Nolan Limited, Dublin, 1920.
8. Mac Ginley ,T.C., The Cliff Scenery of South-Western Donegal, pg 46, Reprinted by Four Masters Press, Dublin, 2000
9. AFM – *Annals of the Kingdom of Ireland by the Four Masters, f from the earliest period to the year 1616,* 7 Vols, Dublin, 1856
10. Mc Gill, Patrick, History of the Parish of Ardara, pg 40, Donegal Democrat, Ardara, Co Donegal.

Chapter 6

1. Aegis Archaeology Reports 2, Excavation of a Post-Medieval Settlement at Rough Point, Killybegs, County Donegal, Frank Coyne and Tracey Collins 2004, pg 9,
2. ibid pg 51

Grave inscriptions

Asken See Brown

Atherton
Sacred
to the memory
of
William Henry
Atherton
Died 5th October 1837
Aged 37

Banks
In memory of
Lieutenant Thomas Banks
of his Majesty's Navy
who died March 13th 1807
in the command of
Maulinbeg Signal Station
He was born August 24th 1777
had been in the service of his
Country from his sixteenth year
and bore a part in Lord
Viscount Duncans glorious
victory over the
Dutch Fleet 11th October 1797

Black
Here lies the body of
Elizabeth Black who departed
this life June 12th 1783 aged 80
years in Pace Requiescat
Also
the body of Francis Black
who departed this life 28th day of
May 1789 Aged 76 years

Blain
The mortal remains of
Margaret Blain
Repose here
she died on 19th March 1847
Aged 80 Years
Also of Charles eldest son of
William Blain
who departed this life
on the 30th January 1850
aged 24 years

"He cometh forth like a flower
and is cut down
he fleeth also as a shadow
and continueth not"
Pheobe Blain
wife of
William Blain
died January 3rd 1873
Aged 75 Years

Blain
Sacred to the memory
of
William Blain
Who departed this life
on Saturday 16th December 1848
Aged 49 years
"The memory of the
just is blessed"
Edward Blain
son of
William and Pheobe Blain
died June 24th 1878
Aged 47 Years

Blain

Here lies the
body of George
Blain who dep
arted this life
September the
26th in the 64
years of his
age Anno
Domini 1721

Blain

Underneath
are the mortal remains
of
George Blain
Who Died July 1792 Aged 60 years
Also Charles Blain his brother
Who died January 1st 1822 Aged
66
Also Thomas Blain son of
the said George Blain
who died in Killybegs 14th July
1845 Aged 63 Years
And in respect of whoes memory
this stone was erected
by a friend

Brice

In memory of Michael
Brice Who departed
June 17th 1781
Aged ?? Also the body of William
Brice
who departed
this life 11th March 1785
Aged 70 years

Brown

Underneath repose the
remains of Margaret
Brown who departed
this life June 2nd 1847
in the 44th year of her
age

Brown

Here lyeth The Body of
Mary Brown alias Asken
Who Departed This life
November The 5th 1742
Aged 70 Years
This monumt was erected
by Archibald Brown foe
his father George
Brown who departed
This life May 6th 1758
Aged 74 years

Carr

Erected to the memory of
James Carr who died
April 18th 1847 by his
sons in America Aged
70 years Requiescant in pace
amen

Conwell

Here lieth the body of
Conell Conwell who
Dep this life 1 of Aug,,1817
Aged 56 years

Grave inscriptions

Conwell
Sacred to the memory
of Mary Conwell
Who departed this life
The 27th February 1847
Aged 69 years
Also
Anthony Conwell
Who died 11th January 1864
Aged 80 years

Devenny
Here lyeth the bo
dy of Mary Devan
Ny Who Departed
This Life J
1740
Aged 59

Dobin
Doth lie the body of Jo
Hn Dobin who departed
this life and was ????
Understone this stone
Aged 36 years
The 23   ???? 1784

Finison
Here lyeth the body of
Patrick Finison Being
74 years of age dis
ceased the 24 of April
Annio Domini 1703
Here in this tomb Aprovest
He was Both Pious Just and
True he was both pleased and
where the good hand of just
ice did peak and when his time
with years was spent The
Corporation did Lament

Gay
John Gay who depart
ed this life February
the 3? 1784 Aged
79 years

Gallagher
Sacred to the memory
of Francis Gallagher
who departed this life
on the 04 of September 1856 (36?)
Aged 88 years

Greenlaw

This tomb was erected
by Robert G
Reenlaw for his fat
her Alexander who de
parted this life Feb 26th
Aged 46

Greenlaw

In memory of
A.R. Greenlaw
The only beloved son of
Aaron and Susanna
Greenlaw who Fell Asleep
in Jesus in the
22nd year of his age
December 18th 1902
Castlereagh

Hamilton

Here lieth the body
of James Eldest son of
James Hamilton of Fintragh Esq
who departed this life
25 Sep 1811
Aged 50 years

Hamilton

Here lieth the body of
James Hamilton who dep
This life on the 12th February
1813 Aged 32
Also
In Memory of William
Who departed this life on the 25
day of
November 1832 Aged 54 years

Hamilton

Here lieth the body
of Richard Hamilton Esq
of Fintragh
who departed this life
the 22nd day of April 1817
Aged 43 years
Also the body of his
daughter Hannah Hamilton
who departed this life on
the 4th day of May 1816
aged 12 years
This stone is erected to their memory
by Ann Hamilton
the affectionate
Wife of the
said Richard

Hamilton

Here lieth the body
of
James Hamilton Esq
of Fintragh
Who departed this life on
the 15th day of may 1815
aged 93 years

Hegarty

Erected by
James Hegarty to the
Memory of his beloved
Wife Catherine Quinn
who departed this life
21st day of June 1858
Aged 36 years

Grave inscriptions

Henderson
Underneath are entered the
remains of the late James
Henderson Esq who dep this life at
Killybegs January
26th 1836 aged 72 years

Jones
Sacred to the memory
of Margaret Jones
Wife of
James Jones of Rushen
She died October 23rd 1819
Aged 65 Years

Kelly
Sacred
to the memory of Mary Kelly
the dearly beloved wife of
Hugh Kelly who departed
this life July the 10th 1869
Aged 74 years

Kennedy
Sacred
to the memory of
Patrick Kennedy
of Firbrega
who departed this
life on the 17th day of
April 1856 Aged 62
Years
This stone was erected
by his son
Charles Kennedy

Kennedy
Sacred
to the memory of
Mary Kennedy
of Firbrega
who departed this life
on the 12th day of November
1855 Aged 52 Years
This stone was erected
by her son
Charles Kennedy

Laphel
Sarah Elis Laphel
Born The 16th November 1838
Departed This life 21 of November
?

Lindsey
Here lyeth the body of
John Lindsey
Being 27 years
Deceased the 30 day of June
Ano Dom 1685
Long See Teelin

Magee
Sacred to the memory
of Mary Magee
Who departed this life February
the 14th 1804 Aged 84 years Also
her
Husband Alexander Magee who
departed this life
August 8th 1804 aged 82 years
Also to the memory of Mary Magee
their Daughter
Who departed this life January 12th

1811 Aged 38 years

Magee
Sacred to the memory
of William Magee
And of Ann Magee his wife
the former died January 31st
1811 aged 84 years and the latter
died October the 12th 1812 Aged
74 years

Mathews
To the memory of
Catherine
Daughter of Alexander
and Isabella Mathews
who departed
This life
January 27th 1858
aged 29 years
"Blessed are the dead
which die in the lord"
McCarty see McLean

McCloskey
In memory
of
John McCloskey who departed this
life
May the 9th 1850 Aged
63 years he lived beloved
and died lamented and remembered
A man more just or true
to trust he has not left
behind

Grave inscriptions

McCloskey
Here lieth the body
of
Patrick McCloskey
who departed this life
July the 19th 1818 Aged 63 years
Also
Ellenor and Fay McCloskey his
Grand daughters
who died in infancy
allo his wife Mary McCloskey
who died Oct the 26th 1832 Aged
78 Years and also the remains of
his son
James McCLoskey who departed
this life April 22nd 1839 aged 15
years

Mc Doel
Sacred
to the memory
of
Henry McDoel
ESQUIRE
who departed this life
on the 20th day of March
1801 Aged 68 years

McFadien
Underneath this stone
lyes the body of
Feragal McFadien
Departed this life
February 4th 1806
Aged 3 years This st
one erected by Feragal McFadien
his father

Grave inscriptions

McGhee

Sacred
to the memory
of
Andrew McGhee
of Killybegs who
departed this life
April the 22nd AD
1815 aged 77 years

McGill

Erected to the memory of
Cornelues McGill
Who departed this life 29th
March 1847 aged 47 years also
His wife Mary McGill
Who departed this life
On 8th January 1860 Aged 37
years

McGuinnis

Here lyeth the
body of John McGuinnis
Who departed this life
June this 1841
Aged 63 years

McHugh

Sacred to the memory
of Philip McHugh who
Died March the 3rd
1816 aged 80 years

McIntyre

Erected in memory
of
William McIntyre
Who departed this life

March 30th 1832 aged 65 years

McLaughlin

Sacred
to the memory of
James McLaughlin
Who Departed this life on
the 16th day of March 1837
aged 34 years

McLean

Sacred to the memory of Mary
McLean
the beloved wife of
Michael McCarthy cg
Who departed this life
the 27th of Decbr 1857
Aged 29 years

Meigan

Sacred
to the memory of
James Meigan of Killybegs and
in York who departed this life
on 2nd Sept 1857 aged 28 years
Also
Patrick Meigan who departed this
life 5th May 1858 aged 78 years
Also
Kate Meigan in religion
Tiressa Joseph of Mt St Vincent
in York who departed this
life June 1862 aged 24 years
Requisescant in pace

Mitcheal
Erected by Jas
Mitcheal in memory
of his son John who
departed this life
November 29th 1840
aged 34 years Also his
brother Wilm. As Above
Aged 21 years

Montgomery
Sacred to the memory of
Grizzell Montgomery
Who Dept this life the
First day of July 1806
Aged 32 years

Morrison
Here lieth the
Body of Mathew
Morrison Who de
parted this life
March the 12th 1836
Aged 62 years

Morrison
here lieth the
body of James Morrison
who departed this life
February 6th 1826 Aged 65 years

Murray
here lieth The Body of
Capt. Jas Mvrray Who Dyed
May 19th 1752 AgeD 40
Years

Nesbitt
Here lieth the body of
Alexander Nesbit
Son of N Nesbit
of Drimannew who died
May the 15th 1719

O'Boyle
Here lieth the body
of Ann O Boyle who
departed this life
Nov 2nd 1808
Aged 18 years

Pallock
Sacred
to the memory
of
William Pallock
Who Departed this life
April the 16th 1833
Aged 28 years
Quinn See Hegarty

Teelin
Here lies the body of William
Teelin who departed this life
August the 1st 1785
Aged 43 years
This stone was erected by
Anne Long alias Teelin
for her husband

Flora and Fauna

Common Name	Latin Name	Irish Name
Flowers		
Creeping Buttercup	Ranunculus repens	Fearbán (reatha)
Lesser Celandine	Ranunculus ficaria	Grán arcáin
Marsh Marigold	Caltha palustris	Lus buí Bealtaine
Wild Turnip	Brassica rapa	Tornapa fiáin
Wavy Bitter-cress	Cardamine flexuosa	Searbh-bhiolar casta
Hairy Bitter-cress	Cardamine hirsuta	Searbh-bhiolar giobach
Cuckooflower	Cardamine pratensis	Biolar gréagáin
Field Pepperwort	Lepidium campestre	Piobracas léana
Common Scurvygrass	Cochlearia officinalis	Biolar trá
Allseed	Radiola linoides	Gathán Lín
Perforate St John's-wort	Hypericum perforatum	Beathnua
Square-stalked St John's-wort	Hypericum tetrapterum	Beathnua fireann
Tutsan	Hypericum androsaemum	Meas torc allta
Slender St Johm's-wort	Hypericum pulchrum	Beanthnua baineann
Common Dog-violet	Viola riviniana	Fanaigse
Ragged-Robin	Lychnis flos-cuculi	Lus síoda
Common Chickweed	Stellaria madia	Flíodh
Lesser Stitchwort	Stellaria pallida	Tursarraing Bheag
Bog Stitchwort	Stellaria alsine	Tursarraing Mhóna
Common Mouse-ear	Cerastium fontanum	Cluas luchóige
Sticky mouse ear	Cerastium glomeratum	Cluas Luchóige Ghreamaitheach
Procumbent Pearlwort	Sagina procumbens	Na bpéarlaí sínte
Herb-Robert	Geranium robertianum	Ruithéal rí
Doves Foot Crane Bill	Geranium molle	crobh Bog
Cut-leaved Crane's-bill	Geranium dissectum	Crobh giobach
Wood-sorrel	Oxalis acetosella	Seamsóg
Common Gorse	Ulex europaeus	Aiteann gallda
Red Clover	Trifolium pratense	Seamair dhearg
White Clover	Trifolium repens	Seamair bhán
Bush Vetch	Vicia sepium	Peasair fhiáin
Common Vetch	Vicia sativa	Peasair chapaill
Meadow Vetchling	Lathyrus pratensis	Peasairín Buí
Bitter Vetch	Lathyrus montanus	Corra Meille
Black medick	Medicago Lupulina	Drúmheidi
Birds- Foot- Trefoil	Lotus corniculatus	Crobh Éin
Field Rose	Rosa arvensis	Rós léana
Bramble	Rubus fruticosus agg	Dris
Tormentil	Potentilla erecta	Néanfartach
Silverweed	Potentilla anserina	Briosclán
Barren Strawberry	Potentilla sterilis	Sú talún bréige
Wild Strawberry	Fragaria vesca	Sú talún fiáin

Flora and Fauna

Common Name	Latin Name	Irish Name
Meadowsweet	Filipendula ulmaria	Airgead luachra
Wood Avens	Geum urbanum	Machall coille
Opposite-leaved Golden-saxifrage	Chrysosplenium oppositifolium	Glóiris
English Stonecrop	Sedum anglicum	Póiríní seangán
Navelwort	Umbilicus rupestris	Cornán caisil
Broad- leaved Willowherb	Epilobium montanum	Saileachán sléibhe
Great Willowherb	Epilobium hirsutum	Saileachán mór
Marsh Willowherb	Epilobium palustre	Saileachán corraigh
Enchanter's-nightshade	Circaea lutetiana	Fuinseageach
Common Nettle	Urtica dioica	Neantóg
Pignut	Conopodium majus	Cúlarán
Marsh Pennywort	Hydrocotyle vulgaris	Lus na pingine
Dock	Rumex obtusifolius	Copóg
Primrose	Primula vulgaris	Sabhaircán
Yellow Pimpernell	Lysimachia nemorum	Lus Cholm Cille
Bog Pimpernell	Anagallis tenella	Falcaire Corraigh
Bittersweet	Solanum dulcamara	Drémire gorm
Common Figwort	Scrophularia nodosa	Cnapánach
Foxglove	Digitalis purpurea	Lus mór
Germander Speedwell	Veronica chamaedrys	Anuallach
Thyme-leaved Speedwell	Veronica serpyllifolia	Lus an treacha
Heath Speedwell	Veronica officinalis	Lus cré
Blue Water- speedwell	Veronica anagallis-aquatica	Biolar grá
Wall speedwell	Veronica arvensis	Lus cré balla
Hedge Woundwort	Stachys sylvatica	Créachtlus
Selfheal	Prunella vulgaris	Duán ceannchosach
Early Forget-me-not	Myosotis ramosissima	Lus míonla luath
Ribwort Plantain	Plantago lanceolata	Slánlus
Sheeps Bit	Jasione montana	Duán Na gCaorrach
Common Marsh-bedstraw	Galium palustre	Rú Corraigh
Common Cleavers	Galium aparine	Garbhlus
Groundsel	Senecio vulgaris	Grúnlas
Oxeye Daisy	Chrysanthemum leucanthemum	Nóinín mór
Daisy	Bellis perennis	Nóinín
Pineapple Mayweed	Matricaria matricarioides	Lus na hiothlann
Black Knapweed	Centaurea nigra	Mullach Dubh
Dandelion	Taraxacum officinale	Caisearbhán
Nipplewort	Lapsana communis	Duilleog Mhaith
Beaked Hawk's Beard	Crepis vesicaria	lus cúráin gobach
Mouse-ear Hawkweed	Pilosella officinarum	Searbh Na Muc
Smooth Sow-thistle	Sonchus oleraceus	Bleachtán mín
Prickly Sow Thistle	Sonchus asper	Bleachtán colgach
Bluebells	Hyacinthoides non-scriptus	Coinnle corra

Flora and Fauna

Common Name	Latin Name	Irish Name
Yellow Iris	Iris pseudacorus	Feileastram
Lords-and-Ladies	Arum maculatum	Cluas chaoin
Common Spotted Orchid	Dactylorhiza fuchsii	Nuacht bhallach
Heath Spotted Orchid	Dactylorhiza maculata	Na Circíní
Redshank	Polygonum persicaria	Glúineach
Devil's- bit Scabious	Succisa pratensis	Bhallach
Purple Loosestrife	Lythrum salicaria	Créachtach
Eyebright	Euphrasia nemorosa	Glanrosc

Ferns

Common Name	Latin Name	Irish Name
Bracken	Pteridium aquilinum	Raithneach
Male Fern	Dryopteris filix-mas	
Broad Buckler Fern	Dryopteris dilitata	Raithneach Chaol
Scaly Male Fern	Dryopteris affinis	Raithneach Ghainneach
Hard Fern	Blechnum spicant	Raithneach Crua
Hartstongue	Phyllitis scolopendrium	Creamh muice fiadh
Lady Fern	Athyrium filix-femina	Raithneach Mhuire
Common Polypody	Poylpodium vulgare	Scim Chaol
Rusty Back	Ceterach officinarum	Raithneach Rua
Maidenhair Spleenworth	Asplenium trichomanes	Dubh-chosach
Black Spleenwort	Asplenium Adiantum-nigrum	Fionncha dubh

Grasses

Common Name	Latin Name	Irish Name
Perennial Rye-grass	Lolium perenne	Seagalach
Crested Dog's-tail	Cynosurus cristatus	Coinfhéar
Black Bent-grass	Agrostis gigantea	
Common Bent-grass	Agrostis tenuis	Beinteach choitann
Tufted Hair-grass	Deschampsia caespitosa	Giofhéar
Yorkshire Fog	Holcus lanatus	An chin bháin
Creeping Soft Grass	Holcus mollis	
Purple Moor-grass	Molinia caerulea	Fionnán
Cocksfoot	Dactylis glomerata	Garbhfhéar
Wood Meadow-grass	Poa nemoralis	
Smooth Meadow-grass	Poa pratensis	Cuise

Rush

Common Name	Latin Name	Irish Name
Common Spike Rush	Eleocharis palustris	Luachair

Trees

Common Name	Latin Name	Irish Name
Hazel	Corylus avellana	Coll
Sycamore	Acer pseudoplatanus	Crann bán
Ash	Fraxinus excelsior	Fuinnseóg
Blackthorn	Prunus spinosa	Draighean
Hawthorn	Crategus monogyna	Sceach geal
Elder	Sambucus nigra	Trom
Elm	Ulmus glabra	Leamhán

Common Name	Latin Name	Irish Name
Eared Willow	Salix aurita	Saileach
Goat Willow	Salix caprea	Saileach
Grey Willow	Salix cinerea	Saileach
Ivy	Hedera helix	Eidhneán

Birds

Black Bird	Turdus merula	Lon dubh
Black Headed Gull	Larus ridibundus	Creanndubh faoileáil
Blue Tit	Parus caeruleus	Meantán gorm
Bullfinch	Phrrhula pyrrhula	Corcrán
Chaffinch	Fringilla coelebs	Bricín Beatha
Coal Tit	Parus ater	Meantán dubh
Dunnock	Prunella modularis	Riabhóg
Goldcrest	Regulus regulus	Dreóilin easpoig
Glaucous Gull	Laus hyperboreous	Faoiléan glas
Goldfinch	Carduelis carduelis	Lasair choille
Great black backed gull	Larus marinus	Droma duibh faoileán
Great Tit	Parus major	Meantán gorm
Greenfinch	Carduelis chloris	Glasán darach
Grey Heron	Ardea cinerea	Corr éisc
Grey Wagtail	Motacilla cinerea	Liath glasóg
Herring Gull	Larus argentatus	Faoileán scadán
Hooded Crow	Corvus corone cornix	Feannóg
House Martin	Delichon urbica	Gabhlán binne
Iceland Gull	Larus glaucoides	
Jackdaw	Corvus monedula	Cág
Kestrel	Falco tinnunculus	Gaoithe
Kittiwake	Rissa tridactyla	saibhéar
Lesser Black backed Gull	Larus fuscus	Druimneach Bheag
Linnet	Carduelis cannabina	Gleóiseach
Magpie	Pica pica	Meaig
Meadow Pipit	Anthus pratensis	Riabhóg Mhóna
Mistle Thrush	Turdus viscivorus	Smolach mor
Mute Swan	Cygnus olor	Eala bhalbh
Oyster catcher	Haematopus ostralegus	Roilleach
Pied Wagtail	Motacilla alba	Glasóg shráide
Redpoll	Carduelis flammea	Deargéadan coiteann
Redshank	Tringa totanus	Cosdearg
Reed Bunting	Emberiza schoeniclus	Gealún giolcaighe
Robin	Erithacus rubecula	Spideóg
Rock Pipit	Anthus petrosus	Chladaigh
Rook	Corvus frugilegus	Préachán
Sedge Warbler	Acrocephalus schoenobaenus	Ceólaire cíbe
Shag	Phalacrocorax aristotelis	Seaga

Flora and Fauna

Common Name	Latin Name	Irish Name
Song Thrush	Turdus philomelos	Smólach
Spotted Flycatcher	Muscicapa striata	Culire liath
Starling	Sturnus vulgaris	Druid
Swallow	Hirundo rustica	Fáinleog
Turnstone	Arenaria interpres	Piar
Willow Warbler	Phylloscopus trochilus	Ceólaire sailighe
Wren	Troglodytes troglodytes	Dreoilín

Mammals

Woodmouse	Apodemus sylvaticus	Luchóg
Rabbit	Oryctolagus cunniculus	Coinín
Daubenton's bat	Myotis daubentoni	Sciathán leathair
Grey seal	Halichoerus grypus	Rón glas

Butterflies

Green-veined White	Artogeia napi	Bánóg
Large White	Pieris brassicae	Bánóg mhór
Small White	Artogeia rapae	Bánóg bheag
Orange-tip butterfly	Anthocharis cardamines	Barr buí
Peacock butterfly	Inachis io	Cearc phéacóige
Small Copper	Lycaena phlaeas	Copar beag
Ringlet	Aphantopus hyperantus	Fáinneog
Meadow Brown	Maniola jurtina	Donnóg

Spiders

Garden Spider	Araneus diadematus	Damhán alla

Insects

Bristletail	Petrobius maritimus	Ghuaireach
Daddy-Long-Legs	Tipula paludosa	Galán
Black Garden Ant	Lasius niger	Capaill
Buff-Tailed bumble bee	Bombus terrestris	Fhiáin beach
Cockchafer	Melolontha melolontha	Cearnamhán
7-Spot Ladybird	Coccinella 7-punctata	
Ashey-Grey Slug	Limax cinereoniger	Seilide liath
Netted Slug	Deroceras reticulatum	Seilide
Common Woodlouse	Oniscus asellus	Fíniúna
Common Earthworm	Lumbricus terrestris	Péist talún

c. 3000 BC: Court tombs erected at Benroe, Carricknamoghill, Cashelcummin and Drumanoo.

c. 2500 BC: Portal tomb erected at Gilbertstown.

c. 2000 BC: Wedge tombs erected at Largynagreana and Roshin.

c. 6th century: Monastic Cells "Na Cealla Beaga" were erected.

c. 500 - 1000AD: erection of Ringforts on prominent hilltops around Killybegs Harbour

1111: Foundation of Raphoe Diocese.

1307: First record listing of the Parish of Killybegs.

1329: Patrick Mc Monagle became Bishop of Raphoe and Rector and Parish Priest of Killybegs.

1355: Bishop Patrick Mc Monagle constructed a manor house at Killybegs (Kit's Castle).

1366: Bishop Patrick Mc Monagle died.

1400/1500: St Catherine's Church was built.

1429: Parishes of Killybegs and Killaghtee united.

1500/1600: The transept was added to St Catherine's Church.

1513: The O'Malley Pirates from Clare Island led by Eoghan O'Malley attacked Killybegs with three war galleys, plundered and burned the town to the ground and took many inhabitants prisoner while Niall Mor (chieftain) and fighting men were absent. Brian Mc Swyne and a party of shepherds and farmers overtook O'Malley's war galleys and slew him and 120 others, captured two of the war ships and rescued the prisoners on board.

Killybegs Timeline

1516/17: A French Knight (who came as a pilgrim to Lough Derg) promised to send O'Donnell a ship with "great guns" to arrive at Killybegs.

1524: Niall Mor died at his castle at Rahan on December 14th, his headstone is preserved at St Mary's Catholic Church.

1533: Resident of Kits Castle, Bishop Elect O'Higgins blessed the sea off Killybegs because the fish had disappeared. After blessing the water, the abundance of herring and sprat returned. O Higgins later fled Killybegs after falling out of favour with Hugh Dubh O Donnell, Chieftain of Tir Conaill.

1543: Killybegs was mentioned as one of the principal Irish havens in a report to Henry VII.

1550: Rory Ballagh plundered and burned the town of Killybegs because O'Donnell refused him the "Overlordship" of Tir Bannagh.

1556: Philip of Spain payed Queen Elizabeth one thousand pounds per-annum to fish Irish waters.

1560: Killybegs native, Donald Mac Gonigle visited Rome on matters connected to the Diocese.

1562: Donald Mac Gonigle was consecrated Bishop in Rome. Bishop Mac Gonigle attended Council of Trent.

1563: Bishop Mac Gonigle returned to Killybegs and made Kits Castle the official seat of the Bishop of Raphoe.

1588: Year of the Armada, Oct 26th
The Girona left Killybegs "with as many of the Spaniards as she could carry". Two/Three days later the ship went down and left only nine survivors.

1589: September 29th, Bishop Mc Gonigle died in Killybegs.

1591: Niall O'Boyle consecrated Bishop of Raphoe and took up residence in Kits Castle.

1592: Red Hugh O' Donnell inaugurated chieftain of Tir Conaill.

1594/1603: The Nine years war.

1596: Bishop O' Boyle wrote a letter to the King of Spain and thanked him for the help he promised to send. Alonso de Cobos, an envoy from the King of Spain, arrived in Killybegs.

1597: Don Roderigo de Vayen, sent by King of Spain, landed at Killybegs, went to Donegal to meet O' Donnell, and was entertained there and showered with presents.

1600: Spanish Ambassador, Ferdinand of Barranova, and Archbishop of Dublin Matthew de Ovidio came to Killybegs, met with O' Neill and O' Donnell and discussed the landing of the Spanish Army to assist the Irish leaders.

1602: Battle of Kinsale.
Red Hugh died.
Kits Castle abandoned.
Bishop O' Boyle forced to leave Killybegs.

1609: An Inquisition was held at Lifford to clarify the extent of church lands in the county.

c1609: The Crown confiscated Mc Swynes estate.

1609: James Hygate became the first protestant curate of Killybegs. Mc Swyne Banaght was indicted & equitted for entering Killybegs with sixty or eighty men in a " warlike manner" on the day Derry was burnt.

1609/1610: First civilian planters arrived in Killybegs.

Killybegs Timeline

1611: Bishop O' Boyle died and was buried on Inishkeel Island (Narin).

1615: By order of King James I, the new borough town of Killybegs was established. Roger Jones was the first Provost (Mayor). Protestant's use St Catherine's Church.

1622: William Hamilton, first Protestant Rector of Killybegs built a new house near the church.

1622: St Catherine's Church was described in royal commission as newly "re-edified and well-repaired".

1627: In March five ships reputed to be pirates came into Killybegs.

1633: Last inaugurated Chieftain of Bannagh died.

1638: The Church of Ireland's Bishop of Raphoe leased the church lands of Killybegs for a term of 56 years to Archibald Erskine.

1641/1653: "1641 Rebellion".

1641: Battle of Stragar, Turlogh Roe O'Boyle of Kiltoorish and the sons of Donough Mc Swyne attempted to recapture Killybegs but were beaten back by forces under the command of Rev Andrew Knox.

1642: English Soldiers evacuated Killybegs.

1642/48: Friars from Donegal stayed in St Catherine's Church.

1648: Cootes troops occupied Killybegs after their recapture of the town sometime in 1648.

1654: The Civil Survey was carried out.

1654/56: The Church was repaired.

1659: The Census Of 1659 showed "Ye Old Town of Killybegs" had 11 English and Scottish and 20 Irish people. In the Killybegs

Corporation it also showed 10 English and Scottish and 21 Irish people.

c.1660-1672: White House was built.

1685: Earliest recorded grave in St. Catherine's Graveyard – John Lindsey.

c.1700/90: The Nesbits started a whaling industry from Killybegs.

1729: Two Killybegs' ships set sail for America with passengers who had indentured themselves and their families for three/four years to pay their passage.

1733: The Church is recorded to be "in good order and seated – the aisles and floor at communion table are flagged".

1743: The big storm blew the thatched roof off The White House.

c.1760: A "great road" was laid out from Killybegs to Ardara

1763: A Catholic Church was built where the old Niall Mór School now stands.

1765: The Nesbitts' ship, "The Bustle", was forced from the moorings and then stranded during a great storm in early April.

1788: The earliest record of a meeting of Select Vestry in St. Catherine's old church.

1790: James Hamilton and Robert Nesbitt superintended the re-slating of the church roof.

1793: The Church of Ireland Vestry decided to enlarge the window below the pulpit.

1801: Henry Mc Doel was killed in a storm and buried in St. Catherine's graveyard.

Killybegs Timeline

1819: Robertson School, Killybegs was built.

1828: St. John's was consecrated and dedicated to on June 6.
St Catherine's Church was abandoned.

1829: Ardara was made an independent parish by the Protestant Bishop
of Raphoe, Killybegs lower went to form part of this new parish.

1834: The Glebe house was built.

1839: Rector William Lodge entered folklore as the leading villain in the
filling of St Catherine's Well.

1843: First mass celebrated in St. Mary's Church.

1845: July the 22nd Alexander Murray, Esq. Of Broughton, died in the
White House after arriving in Ireland only a few days earlier.

1845-1850: The Great Famine.

1853: Murray Steward built Kelly's Quay.

1864: Roshine School was built.

1864: Murray Stewart provided two pieces of land for a new graveyard,
transferred to the parish on July 22nd.

1869: Church lands reverted to the government at the time of the disestablishment of the Church of Ireland.

1872: The catholic graveyard was opened on August the 4th.

1894: Alexander Duthie (Aberdeen fish trader) was fishery Inspector for
Donegal, he set up lessons on boat building and net mending in
Killybegs.

Killybegs Timeline

1897: Congested District Board built the pier at a cost of £10,000.

1898: Industrial school was built.

1900: Ayrshire carpet manufacturers Messrs Morton & Co. established a factory in Killybegs.

1935: Mr James Mc Leod arrived in Killybegs with a 45'0 seine net vessel; "Martha Helen" It instituted a new development in Killybegs fishing.

c. 1936: Gate and wall built around St Catherine's Well.

1940: Industrial School was evacuated and used as a military barracks until 1945.

1943: V.H. Lavery, A sailor in the Royal Navy is the last burial in St Catherine's graveyard.

Killybegs today

Bibliography

Aegis Archaeology Reports 2, Excavation of a Post-Medieval Settlement at Rough Point, Killybegs, County Donegal, Frank Coyne and Tracey Collins 2004

AFM – *Annals of the Kingdom of Ireland by the Four Masters, from the earliest period to the year 1616*, 7 Vols, Dublin, 1856.

Centenary Committee, Cententary of The Church of the Sacred Heart, pg 37, Mountcharles, Ballyshannon, 1997.

Conaghan, Charles, *The History and Antiquities of Killybegs*, Ballyshannon, 1974.

Conaghan, Pat, *Bygones*, Killybegs, 1989

Conlan, Fr Patrick, *The Franciscan Third Order in Donegal*, Donegal Annual, 1997

Doran, Linda, FAS Graveyard Guidelines, 1990.

Gwynn, Aubrey and Hadcock R Neville, *Medieval Religious Houses, Ireland*, London, 1970.

Jefferies, Henry A, *A catalogue of the bishops of Raphoe to A.D. 1600*, Donegal Annual, 1997

Lacy, Brian, *Archaeological Survey of County Donegal*, Lifford, Donegal County Council, 1983.

Livingstone, E, *The Oxford Dictionary of the Christian Church*, Oxford University Press, USA, 1997.

MacGill, P. J, *The Parish of Killaghtee*, 1968.

MacGill, Patrick, *History of the Parish of Ardara*, Donegal Democrat, Ardara, Co Donegal.

Mac Ginley ,T.C, The Cliff Scenery of South-Western Donegal, Reprinted by Four Masters Press, Dublin, 2000.

Maguire, Rev. Canon Edward, A history of the Diocese of Raphoe, Browne and Nolan Limited, Dublin, 1920.

Mallon, M, *St. Catherine's Well*, Dearcadh, Ardara, 1994-95

Silke Fr John J, The Diocese of Raphoe, Catholic Church, Diocese of Raphoe, Letterkenny, 2000.

The earliest photograph of St Catherine's Church, September 1933

Our thanks to Donald Smith for this photograph

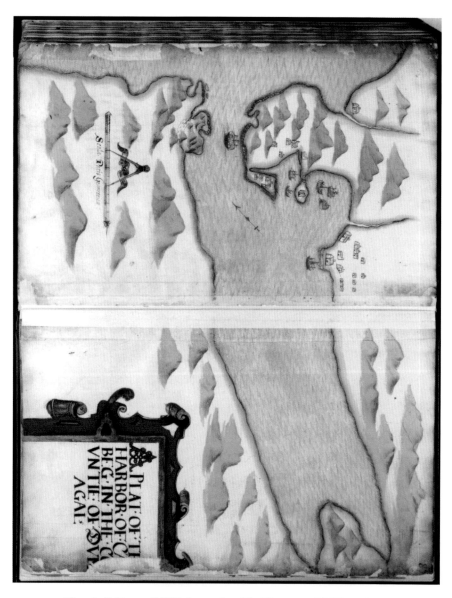

The full Map of Killybegs by Sir Thomas Phillips 1622

Reproduced by kind permission of the Drapers' Company of the City of London

102

Detail of the 1622 map showing the old and new town of Killybegs

Reproduced by kind permission of the Drapers' Company of the City of London

Acknowledgements

We would like to thank the following for their continued help and support during this project and scheme:

FÁS: In particular to Francis Byrne who has been great source of support, advice and belief in the project, John Diver, Ray McEnhill, Una Donnelly, Bridie Sharkey, Chris Magee and Gerry Burton.

Killybegs Employment Project: A big thanks to Tony O Callaghan who played a major role in the project, Also many thanks to Michael Murphy, Fr. Colm Ó Gallchóir, Rev Ken McLaughlin, Fr, Lorcan Sharkey, Colin Mabon, Ann Marie Bourke, Brid Mclean and Marion Mc Guinness.

County Donegal Heritage Office: Joseph Gallagher and Paula Harvey for support and funding.

Many other people who gave time, advice, photographs, information, etc. These include: Eamonn Monaghan, Eugene McHugh, Donald Smith, Donald Martin, Victor Buckley (OPW), Frank Coyne (Aegis Archaeology), Barry Sharkey for providing the archaeological and engineers report, Michael Mooney for providing funding for the lamination of gravestone drawings, Charlie Boyle, Pat Conaghan, Moira Mallon, Helen Meehan, St Catherine's Well Committee, St Catherine's Weekend Committee, the staff of the local and central libraries, Robert Blaine, the Community Employment workers, the Drapers' Company of the City of London for the 1622 map of Killybegs, Dr Raymond Refaussé - Librarian of the RCB library. And to everyone else for their kind support and enthusiasm towards the project.

Last but not least, to every trainee who participated in the project - nothing would have been achieved without you!

Go raibh míle maith agat